COLLEGE PREP GUIDEBOOK

HOW TO ACE HIGH SCHOOL, EXCEL ON THE SAT AND ACT, AND WIN ADMISSION TO THE COLLEGE OF YOUR CHOICE

BY

CHARLES LEWIS, MD MPH

SECOND EDITION

Psy Press ~ Est. 1978

2

Psy Press
Carrabelle, Florida
PsyPress email.com
Edition: 2.1 Sept. 2015
On Demand Publishing
ISBN: 978-1505261578

TABLE OF CONTENTS:

Dedicated to Carla and Mikael,
who inspire me with their multiple geniuses.

The reason a lot of people do not recognize opportunity is because it usually goes around wearing overalls, looking like hard work.
~Thomas Edison

CHAPTER 1: THE PATH TO SUCCESS

You can build castles in the sky if you first build strong foundations on the ground.

~ Khan Abdur Rehman Khan

From the desert valley floor near Lone Pine, the Sierra Nevada rise as a formidable wall of mountains. The tallest of these craggy peaks, Mount Whitney, ascends 14,505 feet into a dazzling electric blue sky; the highest mountain in the continental United States. In a year, only several weeks yield accessibility to climbers, and as a younger man, I had the fortune to surmount it.

It took preparation. I had scaled several 11 to 12 thousand foot peaks in the Rocky Mountains during the preceding month. We camped at an elevation of 8,000 feet to acclimate to the thin air. We selected the day of the full moon to give us extra hours of light if we ran into trouble.

My two brothers and I climbed this craggy peak without pitons, harnesses, carabiners, or ropes; we walked up eleven miles of switchbacks and trails. Admittedly, even with preparation, the

last half mile in the rarefied atmosphere was a trudge. The final
few hundred yards of trail, steep, and over slippery rocks, were
taken slowly, as the dry, thin air, starves the brain and muscles of
oxygen. We had no special abilities, training, or gear for this
adventure; what we had was fun, spectacular vistas, and a great
sense of accomplishment.

Very few people attempt the perilous ascent up the exposed cliff
faces of Mount Whitney; nevertheless, hundreds make the trek
up the backside of the mountain each year. From a distance,
mountains appear steep and insurmountable. However, as you
approach them, most are composed of a series of gently sloping
foothills, followed by some higher prominences. Many of those
are not especially difficult to ascend.

When you look ahead at the challenges required to learn
something difficult, to accomplish a complex task, or achieve
greatness, the tasks may seem intimidating. Like mountains,
many goals in life, which appear daunting, can be achieved by
taking time to find the right route, and being willing to take a
series of steps, with each small step preparing you for the next.

If you have opened this book, you almost certainly have
aspirations. Success can manifest in as many forms as there are
people. It may signify wealth to some, an exemplary life of service
to others, a music career in front of screaming fans, or designing
new cities. Success for you today may be no more than figuring
out how you are going to get your next meal, or if you are reading
this on behalf of your teenage son or daughter, success may be
having them moving forward into independence. This guidebook
will help point out paths that will assist your ascent.

Education is key to success and freedom. Yes, freedom. This is
not a reference to how an educated society promotes and expands
individual liberty. It is about avoiding personal economic
enslavement. Liberty is little comfort when you are struggling to
make ends meet. What good is freedom if you don't have the

economic resources to utilize those prerogatives? If you have a holiday but no money, you don't need a passport. When you're broke, you have little opportunity to utilize freedom, or latitude to explore your dreams.

A purse is but a rag unless you have something in it.

~Ishmael

More relevant than freedom is opportunity. More salient than education, which can take place in non-competitive community colleges, is the favorable environment of a great university that provides opportunities to expand and utilize your talents.

Most of us have interests we never explore and abilities we never utilize as we never gain access to the requisite opportunity. Following the advice provided herein can open doors that would otherwise be missed. Superior class ranking, a great college placement test score, effective letters of recommendation, and knowing how to apply open doors to better schools and scholarships and to opportunities for success that most people never have available to them.

Some of the things required for admission to competitive colleges and scholarships are obvious:

- A high grade point average
- A high SAT or ACT score

College placement tests are one of the highest-returning investments a young person can make for their future. Think of your preparation for the ACT and SAT, and the skill set needed for, them as an *investment*. Time and effort deployed to improve test scores can facilitates admission into more selective schools, and help obtaining funding and scholarships to pay for college as they indicate that the student has superior intellectual prowess.

These college placement tests are used to assess academic aptitude and achievement. However, preparation for these tests is not difficult. The ACT and SAT depend upon a finite knowledge and skill sets that can be learned. Proper preparation can make a significant difference in the test score, moving a student from an "also ran" to a front-runner.

Other things imperative for admissions into the top colleges and for winning scholarships, which are less obvious, but may prove just as important are:

- An excellent, well-prepared application
- Certain extracurricular activities
- Great letters of recommendation
- Individuality and joy that comes across in the paper trail
- Maturity, perseverance, and tenacity
- Mastery in a self-selected area
- Self-confidence
- Passion

This book provides counsel on how to optimize your efforts along your path to success, and guidance to help you attain acceptance to a great college and win scholarships. The goal is to help you avoid inefficient routes filled with drudgery and wasted effort by presenting surer paths facilitate your chances of accomplishing your goals. This book is a guide that maps out safer routes to success so you can thrive and enjoy your high school experience. Some of the secrets provided are:

- How to study more efficiently
- How to earn better grades without working harder
- How to achieve better college placement test scores
- How to, with the same scores, dramatically raise your chances gaining acceptance into an elite university
- How to get your college education paid for
- Avoiding pitfalls that doom many college students
- How to succeed and have fun at the same time

This book is not a guide for posers who hope to bluff, scam, deceive, or fake their way into college or a career. If you want to put lipstick on a pig, look elsewhere. You could Photoshop yourself into a white water raft or onto a mountaintop, but how is that fulfilling? You may snag fugacious virtual flirtations with faked photos, even so, second dates are unlikely if the estate, soft-top Mercedes Roadster, and pearly white teeth are not yours. Some may lie, cheat, and sleep their way to a Harvard degree, but they burn more energy covering their tracks, hiding their ineptness, and waiting on karma than they would have spent developing ability, knowledge, and competence. This book promotes personal development and attainment.

Perhaps you have not been a preeminent scholar. Maybe you are a late bloomer; we don't all mature on the same time scale. Perhaps you attended a failing high school, or even dropped out of high school, but now you have goals and are ready to move forward. The advice provided herein remains germane. Your path may include completing an associate's degree from a two-year community college before applying to a great university. The advice provided here can help with that process as well. You will still need test scores and documentation to apply to college. You can still apply for scholarships to help pay for your education after you get into college.

The best way to make your dreams come true is to wake up.
~Paul Valery

Life isn't about finding yourself. Life is about creating yourself.
George Bernard Shaw

HOW TO READ THIS BOOK: Use this book to practice better reading habits. Mature reader's eyes move across the page capturing groups of words, rather than single words. Each time the eyes move in a saccade; they jump from one group of words to the next. A typical saccade group for good comprehension captures about 15 to 25 characters. This book's printed text is formatted to facilitate the practice of reading with high comprehension and speed. Pay attention to the way you read this book. Try to read using no more than three or four saccades for most lines of text in this book to achieve improved comprehension and speed.

CHAPTER 2: TIME

We are what we repeatedly do. Excellence, therefore, is not an act, but a habit.

~Aristotle

High school is a unique, extraordinary time for most young people. As we near adulthood, we explore what we want for our future. This time is also a special period for brain development, where emotions can be almost tangible. Our energy and passions shape our identity and set the stage for adult life. High school should be a time of exploration, of building social skills, and of building confidence.

Core activities of adolescence include the growth of the body and brain and learning to negotiate interpersonal relationships. It is a time to learn about forging friendships, learning to avoid causing offense, discovering values, developing skills and ascertaining passions. Learning social skills, forming an identity and developing self-confidence are essential tasks of the high school years that shape the young person's future.

There are numerous tasks requiring attention during the high school years, and at best, barely time for the essentials. It can be a mistake to focus too narrowly on educational goals: getting perfect grades, playing sports and musical instruments, volunteer work, and other extra-curricular endeavors that might be done in effort to gain admission into a top college. It is thus essential that time be spent strategically. This doesn't mean you should allocate all your time working diligently. Social activities, play, and friendships are imperative in preparation one for adulthood, and besides, life should be fun. To have ample time for diversions and rest requires using study time efficiently so that there is plenty of time to socialize, relax, and explore.

Keep Your Tools Sharp

Trying to study when you are enervated and fatigued is a waste of time. Cramming for tests may help you pass, but it is unlikely that you will either understand the material or retain it for later use. Your goal should be to form a foundation of knowledge and skills upon which you can build. Cram and forget is not a strategy for educational or skill achievement. Cramming late into the night may avoid a failing grade; however, it does not keep you from failing the underlying objective of your efforts.

Pay attention to what works for you, in order to find the study methods that are most effective for you. It is easy to waste time working without accomplishing any real learning. If you find that after having studied for a while, you are rereading paragraphs and not understanding, or spending more time daydreaming than problem-solving, it may be time to take a break. Most people do not maintain sustained attention from more than 40 minutes. Take breaks: get a snack, walk around, do something else for a few minutes, and then do another stint to get your homework done. Don't waste time spinning your wheels when nothing is being accomplished.

Avoid multitasking; it only allows you to do a mediocre job of multiple things. Turn Facebook, the TV, and phone interruptions off while you study. You can accomplish more in less time when your attention is focused and on track. Catch up with your buddies during breaks, and then turn it off. How many athletes use Facebook or messaging during practice? Would you consider doing algebra homework at a party? Work when you work. Play when you play. Focus on one thing at a time and do it well. You will get your work done more efficiently, and then have more time to enjoy other activities, giving them undivided attention.

It is easy to fall into time-sucking black hole habits that ravenously consume your discretionary time. If you are frittering away two or more hours a day on activities such as TV, Facebook,

MMOG's (Massive Multiplayer Online Games), perusing the internet, or other vacuous diversions, ask yourself if it is a wise use of your time or an addiction. It is easy to squander numerous hours trifling, doing stuff that provides little satisfaction.

Budget your time; it is limited. You could use the thousand hours you might waste in distractions over the next couple of years pursuing mastery of a musical instrument, volunteering, or developing expertise in an area of interest. Use the time to participate in activities you actually enjoy and feel fulfillment from. Budget the amount of time you want to put into these time-sinks such as television, Facebook, and Angry Birds, and then stick to it.

More importantly, figure out when to work and when to lounge. There are times of the day when you are more astute and focused and can better perform the tasks of studying, and other times when you are too distracted or tired to make real progress or do quality work. Use the time of the day when you can focus to study; relax and play during the hours best suited to relaxation.

If you use TV as a strategic allocation of time to chill out, it can still be edifying. Programs such as NOVA, Frontline, TED Talks, or movies of great literature you have read or should have read can inspire, inform, and broaden your perspectives. Do you want to watch programs about denture cream and term-life insurance geared for the infirm geriatric population? Don't let TV filled with commercials sap your time. If you allocate time to TV, use the time you have budgeted to watch commercial free content; get a subscription to HULU, Netflix or Amazon streaming, or watch PBS. Watch programs online, so they fit your schedule; don't build your schedule for entertainment around the TV's schedule.

If you want your brain to function efficiently, treat it with respect. Take care of it; it is your most valuable asset. Eat real food (natural foods, fruits, and vegetables), avoid soda pop, junk food, and fried foods. Get exercise that makes you sweat. Not only will you have a more attractive body and less acne, you will have a healthier brain that focuses more astutely. If you weigh too much, avoid sweet drinks. Studies of young people have shown the most effective weight loss diet is simply avoiding sweet beverages.

Growth hormone is released during sleep, as are many other regulatory hormones. If you want to grow, including having your brain grow new connections, you need sufficient and regular sleep. Newborn babies need about 16 hours of sleep per day, while 80 year-olds may only need six, in part because they are no longer learning much. During adolescence, the body still needs 9 to 10 hours of sleep a day. At age 17, the normal physiologic requirement for sleep is 9.6 hours per 24-hour cycle.

Memory consolidation and integration occur during sleep. If you short-change sleep, you will not learn as well. Reaction time slows, so when you are sleep deprived, you will not perform as well in athletic pursuits or drive as safely. Sure, you may be able to function with less sleep, but your brain will not work as effectively. The amount of sleep required for peak performance is very different from that at which one feels fatigued or tired. If you feel tired, you are probably sleeping 3 hours per night less than that required for peak performance and optimal health. Some sleep deficit can be restored by sleeping a few extra hours on weekends. If you are a high school student, assume that you need 67 hours of sleep per week to function at your best.

Keep in mind that you are competing with other students across the country and globe for seats at select colleges and for limited scholarship dollars. These students are just as smart or smarter, work as hard or harder and are as gifted athletes as you are. Sleep can give you an advantage; lack of sleep can take your advantage away. Sufficient sleep makes us appear healthier and more attractive[1]. Coffee, colas, and other caffeinated beverages may help wake you up or feel more alert, but they do not make up for the loss of sleep time that is required for efficient learning.

Tobacco, drugs, and alcohol are not your friends. Tobacco users do not do as well in school. Marijuana has deleterious effects on the developing brain; teenagers using pot easily lose an average of eight IQ points that never return, while this does not occur from adult use[2]. Drugs and alcohol are the sandlots of losers.

Where to Focus

Fill in gaps in areas where you are weak. Get tutoring if there are areas you don't understand. Often, even a small gap in knowledge can become a major roadblock along the way, and sometimes those gaps are surprisingly small and easy to set right. Many obstacles that look like brick walls turn out to be as flimsy as Styrofoam once you slow down and examine them. The sooner you fill your learning gaps, the more quickly and easily you can progress, get superior grades, and move forward. If there is something you don't understand in class, slow down, get help.

Focus on building a full foundation of math skills. In math, it doesn't pay to jump ahead, or skip areas you find difficult. Missing a few of centuries of ancient history is unlikely to impede your understanding of the American Revolution, but missing math concepts can come back and bite. Mathematics is like a tower; if you have half-baked bricks as a base, it will eventually crumble and collapse.

Focus on writing. Work to develop your skills at writing and communicating clearly and concisely. Focus on mastery of subjects and skills. It is far more useful to be proficient at simple tasks, than incompetent at something difficult. Being proficient builds a foundation upon which you can grow; it builds confidence. When you have self-confidence, you are more likely to step up to more complicated and sophisticated tasks. Success rewards individuals committed to developing great skill in areas they are passionate about, rather than those who flit around, dabbling in one area and then another. Strive for excellence, especially in activities and subjects you enjoy.

Challenge yourself to develop abilities. Just as with computer games or sports, when activities are is too easy, they are boring, and we lose interest. If it is too difficult, we can't compete, and we become apathetic. If we are forced to stay in the game, but lack ability, it causes anxiety and distress. The best place to be is in the sweet spot, the Goldilocks groove, where things are just right. This occurs when your capabilities match the challenge; where skills and knowledge develop at the same speed as the challenge mounts. Challenges that actively utilize our skills and knowledge get us into the "flow," a place of focused engagement, learning and high-level performance. During flow, learning is fun and pleasurable. Good computer game makers and great teachers know this and progressively increase the challenge to keep things interesting, but not too difficult. Try to select classes, teachers, and activities that keep you in the flow.

Usually in the classroom, students in the flow are in the top quarter of the class and earning A's. Seek out classes at an appropriate level where you do well while building your knowledge and skills. This is preferable to struggling in a difficult course, where you are lost. It is nearly as destructive to be in a class that is too easy and not engaging or challenging as to be in one that is out of reach.

Learning should be work, but that work should be engaging, neither dreary or boring nor overwhelming. If you are making an appropriate effort, but find yourself in a class where you are not doing well, ask your counselor if there might be an alternative teacher or class level that is more appropriate for you; where your efforts will provide more progress. Success does not happen on its own. It requires work; however, this work does need not be unpleasant. Work is simply focused activity to accomplish a goal. It can be fun, engaging, and challenging.

A great teacher makes education interesting and accessible. A poor one makes the fascinating dull, the intriguing boring, assigns hours of busy-work, and transforms the material into an esoteric haze; the student might be better off plugging their ears and learning the material on their own. If there is a choice, push to get into the classes with the best teachers available.

Doing the Things You Hate

Often we avoid the subjects we do poorly in or avoid things we feel we are not good at; they are hard for us. Most often this is because we impatient. Sometimes we are missing a few, small, simple areas of understanding, and this can cause difficulties. People often give up, as the area or activity seems burdensome and tiring, causing boredom.

You might be surprised that most skills require less than 20 hours of focused learning to get over the hump. What separates most people from a lifetime of skills, in playing a musical instrument, having facility with math, tennis, or juggling, is that they could not get past the first few frustrating hours of focused practice. By breaking things into manageable and understandable pieces, and working as little as 40 minutes a day, you can have a new skill in a month. Losers never get this far.

Extracurricular Activities

Don't waste time doing things you don't enjoy just to put them on a résumé. Earning merit badges to attain the rank of Eagle Scout may be fun and challenging for you. However, if you would rather be scrubbing chamber pots than camping, use your time to accomplish something else. ROTC or Junior Achievement may open doors for you, but it is unlikely to provide you with any benefit if you think its lame. If you are ambivalent about basketball, don't do it just so that you can look well-rounded.

Many colleges and scholarship programs like to see community service. Volunteer for activities that you enjoy. If your heart is not in it, it is unlikely that you will excel at an activity or want to do it. Participate in activities you enjoy.

If your parents push activity that you don't care for, investigate other ones that interest you and talk to them about the things that excite you. They may push in one direction only because they believe you would enjoy it if you got started, and you might, and because they think it will benefit you. They may not be aware of other opportunities that you would enjoy more and excel in. Your parent may push towards something you have no interest in because they see that you are not getting enough exercise, or activity, but may support you when you suggest a different activity that holds interest for you.

There are millions of kids playing basketball and tens of thousands playing trumpet in marching bands. These activities are unlikely to help you stand out from other students and entice a university to snatch you up. A colossal commitment of time and effort can be consumed in achievement of excellence. If you are going to compete on skill and talent in a crowded field, you need to be exceptional. If you do it because it is a favorite activity, that's great. Few students, however, win music scholarships, and most music scholarships don't cover the cost of education.

If you believe that an athletic scholarship is a great opportunity, read Chapter 11 to see who really wins this game.

The extracurricular activities that selective colleges and scholarship boards value are those that demonstrate empathy or compassion, show that you believe that you can make a positive change in your community and the lives that you touch, demonstrate leadership, or show you have persistence to master a skill. They are looking for individuals who use creativity and leadership to approach and resolve problems. They are not looking for those who work extraordinarily hard (those people burn out), but rather people who use their gifts to pursue extraordinary goals.

Most importantly, your extracurricular activities should be fun and engaging for you. If you can describe your activities with joy and excitement, or with a sense of fulfillment, it tells about you as a person and differentiates you from others. It creates an image far more appealing than just a GPA and test score.

Unless you change direction, you're likely to end up where you're headed.

~Chinese Proverb

CHAPTER 3: WINNING ADMISSION TO A GREAT UNIVERSITY

Standing on the starting line, we're all cowards.

~Alberto Salazar

In the introductory chapter, I pointed out that selective colleges principally base their admissions on three factors:

- Grade point average (GPA)
- College placement test score
- Personal essay

A fourth essential to getting into a highly selective university is:
- The application

Most students spend thousands of hours of work over 4 years on their high school GPA, less than 20 hours over a few days preparing for the ACT or SAT, and a couple of hours the night of the deadline to completing college applications. A surprising number of students wait until May of their senior year to apply to colleges.

There is rampant grade inflation in the United States. A low GPA suggests a lazy, uninspired, dull student that avoids work. A high GPA, however, does not guarantee the inverse: that the applicant is a brilliant, effective student with a creative mind. At one time, a GPA of 3.0 indicated a diligent, intelligent student, and a 3.5 was exceptional. Now, however, a weighted GPA of 4.0 is common. You may attend one of those now rare schools where a 3.5 is exceptional, but this un-inflated GPA will compete against those from kids in failing schools where social promotion is the rule and where bright students sleep through class, learning next to nothing, and still get A's. But don't be jealous;

those in weak school are far worse off, as they are falsely led to believe, by their superior grades that they are performing at a competitive level. When they get to college, they often find that they have not been prepared for college.

Grade inflation has caused colleges and universities to rely much more on the college placement tests than on GPA. An ACT or SAT score is often weighted as much as the GPA. Thus, if you want to get a place in a selective school, plan to put in considerably more than two weeks preparing for these tests.

Don't high school classes prepare you for placement tests? Yes, algebra and geometry do. The math helps, but critical thinking, perseverance, and strategy are just as important. Do the three years of high school English classes help prepare you? If they trained you for error detection, and for correct grammar and punctuation, they may help. Nevertheless, the skills relevant to these tests are often not taught in high school classes; you are already expected to know this material. Many skills tested on the ACT and SAT are not the focus of high school classes. In fact, *most of the material you need to know for these tests is taught in middle school or 9th-grade math and English.*

Conversely, however, preparing for these tests will help you do much better in high school and college. Studying for these tests will make you better at test taking, better at essay writing, and better at problem-solving.

Preparing for the English section and the science, which is just another critical reading section, on the ACT will help you read more strategically; learning grammar and punctuation will help you find errors more easily. Preparing yourself for the math section will help you learn to how to approach difficult problems without obvious answers, and to look at problems from more than one vantage point. Learning to perform well on these tests includes learning to back-checking and making sure that the obvious answers are the correct answers.

Honing these skills can help raise your GPA and assist in other aspects of your life. Preparing early in high school, and not waiting until your junior year when you are about to take the tests, will help you get better grades throughout high school, college and graduate school, as well as improve your placement test scores.

When I was in high school and college, (during the Jurassic period before word processors) and wrote prose, I concentrated on the storyline, the characters, conflicts and capturing my reader's interest. I didn't pay much attention to spelling, proper punctuation, or grammar. My stories were creative and fun, but my teachers only saw errors. I felt that I had accomplished the creative goal, and the rest were minor details, but to the teacher, these details were the assignment. Grammar and spelling are certainly easier to score than creativity. If I had been competent with grammar and punctuation, it would have been little work to get better grades. Studying for these prep tests helps in learning these skills and in using them more automatically. Studying for these tests early in high school helps boost the student's GPA.

The college application essay is the third major component for attaining admission into a college or university of your choice. It demands more than a few hours attention. Write it as if you were going to publish it. It should be error free. It should be ready for publication, and such an enjoyable read that a stranger would read it for pleasure.

Professional writters don't attempt to turn out great works in one evening. Why do so many students think that they can? There are books on how to write your college application essay in 45 minutes. If you are confident that you are guaranteed a seat in the college of your choice, and just need to complete the requisite forms for a college with open admissions, go ahead, do a one-hour essay. If you have an ACT score of 28 for a school that requires an 18, you will probably get in with almost any essay. However, if the admissions are competitive, the essay deserves and requires much more than a couple of hours of work. The same applies to scholarship essays. Essays take time to mature.

A final and essential task required for getting into a great college is applying. It won't happen if you don't do it. I don't know of any academic recruiters that will come to your home and fill out the paperwork for you. In fact, I think of the application as a test in itself. Read the chapter on applying for college long before the application deadline. Reading it the night before applications are due will do little good.

A person who never made a mistake never tried anything new.
~Albert Einstein

Chapter 4: Easy A's

I was always looking outside myself for strength and confidence, but it comes from within. It is there all the time.

~Anna Freud

Getting a high GPA does not require super smarts. If you are a prodigy and can sleep through your AP Calculus, AP Art History and AP Physics classes, and get 5's on the exams, I respect that immensely; you can ignore the following advice.

For most successful individuals, however, it takes cultivation of talent, intellect, and effort to succeed. For most of us, these are not in endless supply. Thus, strategic allocation of these resources is essential for attaining academic ascendance.

When a manager at Toyota asked his workers if they had any ideas of how they could improve productivity. No one spoke up. Then he rephrased the question, asking the workers if they had any ideas for making their jobs easier. There were dozens of useful ideas. The key to getting better grades is not to work harder, but to make learning easier.

I am not suggesting sloth, but rather advocating strategic use of your energies to make learn interesting and enjoyable, rather than laborious or tedious. These are strategies for making learning more effective and productive, with less work.

With the best teachers, you learn a lot, don't struggle and make A's. The goal here is the same; to learn more with less effort, to enjoy learning, and get A's.

Better Grades; Less Work

Here are some strategies, tips, and tricks.

1. Sit in the first or second row of the classroom.
2. Don't just show up; be present and be nice.
3. Get and use the textbook.
4. Review your class work each evening.
5. Do your work sooner than later.
6. Do your homework
7. Use the online grade book.
8. Practice the art of grade engineering.
9. Get help sooner than later.
10. Be organized
11. Be single minded.
12. Stretch, but don't overreach.
13. Don't jam up your brain cramming.

Sit Up Front

Sit in one of the front two rows of seats in the classroom. It is much easier to maintain focus and understand what is being taught in the classroom when sitting up front.

Most classrooms have terrible acoustics. Reflections of sounds off walls and background noise interfere with understanding. It is typical for classrooms to have such bad acoustics that one in four spoken words in unintelligible to students in the middle of the room. Imagine trying to read a textbook in which a quarter of the words were missing or wrong. The further back one sits; the more interference there is to understanding, and the more work it is for the brain to interpret meaning from the context of the lecture.

This extra mental work, even though it may not be conscious, causes fatigue and dissipates attention; not only yours, but those around you. The further back you sit in a classroom, the more likely the students around you are not paying attention to the teacher, are distracted, and distracting each other.

Better-designed classrooms would be great, but until then, sit in one of the two front rows. This is especially important if you are having difficulty understanding, if it is not your first language being spoken, or your hearing is impaired. If seating is assigned, you can ask to be moved. Tell the teacher or your counselor that you are having difficulty focusing or hearing and that you would like to sit closer to the front. If seating is not assigned, you may need to get to class early enough to grab a seat in the front.

Sitting in the front of the classroom helps you focus on the teacher, rather than sitting in the back, daydreaming about stroking the hair of the girl in front of you, or having your mind wander outside into the sunshine beaming in through the window. There are fewer distractions in the first two rows of the classroom. Sit near the best students, who spend less time gossiping and texting during class. This will help you stay focused; you will be more likely to make friends, form study groups, and share class notes with tuned in, successful students.

Make a Footprint

Participation is an important part of a grade in many classes. Make sure you have a footprint in these classes. Let the teacher know that you exist. No meek, halfhearted hand-raising. Reach for the sky, so that the teacher knows you are participating! If you don't know the answers, ask intelligent questions. Don't hide in the back corner or shrink into your seat making yourself small and invisible. Don't snooze. Don't cut class. You want to the teacher to know your name, and associate it with a positive classroom experience. Sitting up front helps make you visible.

Classroom conduct also affects your grades, especially when the difference between grades is just a few points. Some easy strategies for boosting your grades include: sitting near the front of the classroom, doing and submitting all the homework assignments, participating in class discussions, taking good notes, and getting to know your teachers.

Be polite to the teacher and to your classmates.

Don't be a grade weasel, begging and grubbing for grades you haven't earned. Nevertheless, it can facilitate negotiations for an extra half point you may come to need if the teacher sees you as an interested student who does not disrupt class. If your teacher likes you and knows that you care about your grade, they may be able to swing an extra point or an extra credit your way.

Get the Textbook

Many schools try to cut back on the high cost of textbooks. They may have only one set for teaching multiple periods, and you may not be assigned one to take home. These books are also heavy, and you likely don't want to lug several of them home and back in your backpack each day.

Even though you may not get one, almost all high school teachers use a textbook and design their lessons from it. They usually have no choice; as the content of what they teach has been standardized by state governments. If you do not have the book, you will be at a handicap.

Even though the teacher may write the material on the board, you may not be able to read it well, may transcribe it into your notes wrong, or not be able to read your notes later. The teacher may not explain things well, or you may miss what they said as your look out at the lovely clouds drifting by, or be distracted by an attractive classmate. The teacher may not have time to cover all the material during the class hour, and skip items essential to your understanding of the material.

Some schools will give a textbook only if you request it. If they give you the option of getting a book, take it. Some schools will give online access to the book, and this can be a reasonable choice. This also depends on your computer situation. Is the computer in a location that is a good study environment for you? Is it reliable? Do you learn well reading from a screen?

Get the book. Most textbooks are updated every few years, and other than the cover art, the previous editions are usually not much different. Updating textbooks allows publishers to prosper. But how much has the Spanish language or geometry changed in the last 5 years? The previous edition of most textbooks can be purchased as used books on Amazon, usually for less than $5. You may even get two copies and leave one home and the other in your locker at school. Read the textbook. It will make your work easier and help attain better grades.

Review Your Class Work Each Day

The material covered each day in class can usually be reviewed in just a few minutes. If you took notes or were given notes, review them, making sure you understand the material. If the material makes sense, you will understand it, and it is easy for your brain to encode.

It is much easier to remember something you understand than to remember a string of meaningless numbers or symbols. If I say "Get a glass from the cabinet and go to the refrigerator, get the orange juice out, pour four ounces of O.J. into the glass, put the juice away, close the refrigerator door and bring me the beverage," you would likely remember the sequence and instructions. If I instructed you to "please get a zoot from the inga, pring the gaffer, regate the trazon florning and flip four werlings of flamding, gate the florning in the trazon, and trinkle me the sonno," and tested you on it, what would you remember? Until you understand what you are learning, it is nonsense.

The best way to make it easy to get good grades is to learn the material. If you actually understand, it is easy to learn. If you learn this week's material, it will be easier to understand next week's material. If you learn this semester's class content, it will be easier to understand, and get an A in the next semester.

Make sure you understand what has been taught every day. When you go back into the classroom, you will be able to build on that understanding. If you don't understand, you are likely to get more deeply mired as each day passes. The goal is to learn a lot, get a great grade, not suffer nor waste time doing this. It is easier to accomplish the learning and earn superior grades doing the assignments right away.

Do Your Homework

A sad reality of education is that busywork, which does not help you learn, usually gets graded, so you have to do it to get a good grade. In contrast, work you are not graded on is often helpful for learning. Do your homework, even when it is not graded.

It is best to do homework related to material covered in class the same day the material was covered while it is still fresh in your mind, even if not due the next day. This reinforces learning. If it is not due for a week, you may not remember as well, and will not learn the material as effectively, and may not do as well on the assignment. Do your homework and remember to turn in assignments. Even a couple of missed homework assignments can shift an A to a B or a B to a C.

Use the Online Grade Book

Most schools have online grade books that show your grades for assignments, and will show if any are missing. Look at it at least once a week to make sure you have everything turned in, and that the grade posted is the one you earned. If the option is available, set it up to email you each week to alert you of any deficits that may be occurring. It is easy to drop a letter grade in a class from missing a minor assignment that was only a few minute's work. Use the grade book to make sure you are maintaining your desired grade. Use the electronic grade book acts as an early warning system to let you know when things are not going as well as they might in a class, and to get you back on track when spring fever or senioritis kicks in.

Make sure you are getting credit for work that you have turned in and that there are no unexcused absences. Teachers sometimes lose an assignment or mismark one in the computer grade book. You may be surprised that you have an unexcused absence for a sanctioned school event that had you out of class, or for a sick day that the teacher did not get an excused absence notice for. Losing a single assignment or an unexcused absence can sometimes drop your grade. Make sure you are getting the points you have earned and deserve, and that you are not losing points when you should not. If you forgot to turn in an assignment, see if the teacher will accept it late.

Grade Engineering

In most circumstances, an A is an A and a B is a B; thus, a 91 percent gives the same GPA as a 99 percent or a 104 percent, which might be awarded for extra credit work. Plan your efforts to ensure that, if you are in close reach of an A, that you put in the added effort to bring that 89% B to a 90.5% A. If you are getting a 78% in a class, do your very best to bring it up to a B, even if it means an 80.1% B. Remember, in an honors class, that 80.1% B earns is a 3.5-point credit, which is usually good enough to keep you in the running for great colleges and scholarships. Sometimes you may need to reallocate energy away from a class where you are getting a 99% so that you can add points to make the grade in another class. Other times you may want to have more time to do extracurricular activities rather than study.

Working to get perfect scores so that you can be the top in each class can be a waste of effort. Remember that enjoying life, developing social skills, and having time to relax and sleep, are all essentials for present and future success. Attaining grades sufficient to move you to the next goal in life is just one part of the equation. Get your A and be happy. The student with the highest GPA in the school may never attain a score above 92% in a class and may never get the highest score on a test.

This is the 2.5% method. Aim for at minimum of a 92.5%. The two and a half percent allows for a margin of error. However, be careful if you do not do well on finals, if the grade is weighed heavily on the final exam, or if the teacher is known to give tough finals and not grade on a curve. Under these circumstances, you may need a larger margin to prevent your 92.5% average from becoming an 89% after the test. Monitor your grades using the online grade book throughout the semester. Check them often to make sure you are maintaining a 2.5% margin.

It is far better to appear to have succeeded with grace and ease, than to look like you had to struggle to survive. Top schools may take students that are bright, but did not apply themselves; however, they will avoid students that slave to make good grades. They want students that will excel at their school, not ones that will struggle to keep up with their classmates. You should be working and applying yourself to learn. It is strategic, however, to limit yourself to classes where when you apply yourself, you earn an A. The goal is to learn the material well, so that it provides useable skills and knowledge that you can build on. If you are passing with low B's, you likely are leaving many potholes in your abilities that will trip you up later.

Get Help Sooner than Later

Get Tutoring: Don't be afraid to ask for help! Some students, particularly bright ones, seem to think it is a failure if they need to ask for help. No matter how bright you are, there will be times you don't understand the material sufficiently. Sometimes the teacher just explains a concept poorly. Rather than struggle and get a low grade, ask for help. Almost everyone has some gaps in their understanding; the earlier you plug those leaks, the less time you will waste, and the easier it will be to get great grades and build your understanding of the material.

It feels far better to succeed than to struggle. Success builds self-confidence and willingness to try new things; struggling will harm your self-esteem and ability to succeed in the future. You should reach and drive yourself, but it should be to build a strong foundation, not to take high risk or dangerous leaps.

A stitch in time saves nine: get help as soon as you realize that you have a deficit in your understanding; don't let it snowball into a C. Remember, if you don't understand something, you are likely not alone. Ask the teacher to explain again. This will help you classmates to understand as well. Get tutoring if you need it.

Try to avoid ever getting grades of C or lower. If you are doing poorly in class, talk to your high school counselor. You may be better off dropping a class than getting a C. If you fail, or in some schools get a D, you may be able to repeat the class and get a low grade removed. Some schools, however, will not award a grade higher than a C if you previously failed a class, or keep the failing grade on your transcript. Check your school's policy.

Use Organizational Jujitsu

Stay organized. Use organization as jujitsu that allows you to use a small amount of energy to defeat a stronger force. Losing your homework, forgetting an assignment, or spacing out about a test the next morning can cost you your grade. Use an organizer (notebook/calendar) for your papers rather than just stuffing them in your backpack. Have a place where you keep assignments to be turned in, and another place to keep work that has been returned to you from the teacher. Keep a daily calendar and make it a habit of not leaving the classroom without checking, and writing down, any homework assignments.

Get a phone number from a bright female classmate (girls are usually better organized) or friend them on Facebook, so that you have friends in your class to contact in the evening or over weekends if you realize you don't know the homework assignment or need help. Failing that, you can check teacher's website for assignments.

Don't be a cowboy. The self-sufficient, independent loner, riding the range may portray macho strength, but it bodes poorly for academics. Working with classmates to understand difficult concepts helps get past the difficult areas. Facebook study groups can be lifesavers.

Have a monthly calendar with school events and dates (such as when term papers are due) so that you can keep them in mind and not wait until the last minute to work on them. Place a reminder to check your grade online on the calendar so that you remember to do it every week. Keep your work neat and organized so that it is easily legible to teachers, friends and you. Label your work with headings so it easy to sort and find.

Think of your organizer as a brain supplement good for an additional ten IQ points. Treat yourself to an organizer notebook that you like. Make a habit of looking at it before leaving school each day to make sure that you have your assignments and any books or papers you need to complete your work or for study. The students that get the best grades are often not those who are smartest, but rather those with the best organizational skills.

At home, have a place to keep schoolwork that your teachers have graded and handed back to you. Keep them until the end of the semester, storing each class' work separately. Those papers may come in handy as study guides. Also, teachers sometimes lose scores; you may need the assignment to get your credit.

Take the time to look at the work the teacher has handed back to you. If there are points marked off, use the opportunity to learn from your errors and to help get it right for the next time. The next time may be on the final exam or another time when you need to know what your teacher has endeavored to teach. It is just possible that what they want you to learn has some value.

Singletask

You may feel that you are good at multitasking. Studies of Harvard students that think they are good at multitasking show they are wrong about this. All they can really do is do switch their attention between tasks and, as a result, they do multiple things poorly.

The brain has a bandwidth sufficient for 1.6 conversations. Humans can talk and sort of listen, or listen and catch bits of different conversations, or sort of listen and plan on what they want to say, but we do not have sufficient bandwidth for even two conversations. We do not listen well while we are thinking of what we want to say.

In business office situations, workers with desks in an open office design are 60 percent less productive. The reason is that they are constantly distracted by noise and conversations of other people, or interrupted by coworkers and managers. We are most productive when we have a quiet, private space where we can study and do our work free of interruptions for large sufficiently large blocks of time. Find or create a study space that you can reliably get your work done, free of interruptions.

Work Just Above Your Level

Take classes that you can do well in. If you are not in the top 10 percent of high school students, don't load up on AP classes that you're going to struggle through. Sure, on a weighted GPA, a B in an AP class is 4.0 in most schools. But if math is not your thing, an A in an easy math for business class will take up much less time, and be much better than a C in AP Calculus where you are lost and frustrated, wasting many hours trying to catch up with the rest of the class, while you fall behind in other areas. Your goal should be to build a strong foundation, not a shaky one filled with holes. Avoid the misery you will suffer from struggling, and the damaging loss of self-esteem and self-confidence that come with failure. It is far preferable to build knowledge and self-confidence in a class at an appropriate level for you than to overreach and fall flat.

Try to get placed in classes in which you can do well when you do your work, and that stretch you just a bit, but which don't have you struggling, or bored or anxious. You want to be learning, and working in A territory.

Cramming is a B Strategy

Would an athlete put off training until the day before a meet, and then prepare late into the night before by working out? Leaving test preparation to the day before a test and staying up into the wee hours to cram a semester's knowledge base into short-term memory is a workable rescue technique that can assist a lackadaisical student pass a test. It is not an effective way to learn, build understanding, or to get A's semester after semester.

Learn the material throughout the course. Review the material in the days before the test to make sure there are no gapping wholes in your knowledge base, and do a quick review the evening before the test. Get some exercise the day before the test, and get to bed by ten, so that you wake refreshed and your brain is functioning at its best.

Honors Classes

Even if you are somewhat weak in an area, it is usually best to avoid regular classes and enroll in honor level classes. Take honors algebra, as an example, compared to regular algebra. For honors classes, most schools give 4.5 points for an A and a 3.5 for a B. *The secret is that honors classes are often easier.*

Honors classes are populated with better prepared, more mature students. There are fewer distractions, fewer kids with behavioral problems, and fewer spit wads flying through the air to disrupt the class, compared to regular classes. Honors classes usually cover material of similar complexity, but often include subject matter that is more interesting. The teacher spends less time yelling and disciplining disengaged oafs, louts, and vulgarians; allowing the teacher to focus on teaching the material more effectively. The assignments are more likely to be fun and engaging. In honors classes, there may be more opportunity for the teacher to help you through your weak areas as fewer kids will be struggling or defiant. You are more likely to make friends who can help you with study notes if you need them. In regular classes, many of the kids may need help or have zero interest. Think of honors classes as going to a private prep school with more engaged teachers and fewer kids waiting to turn 16 to drop out. Students usually learn more with less work in honors classes than regular classes.

You can attend an excellent high school, and still be in a terrible school if you are assigned classes with kids without aspirations or prospects of attending college. You should actively defend your right to an education that prepares you to meet your aspirations. Don't allow counselors to place you below your level or in classes where learning is not taking place. If you have not been a star in the past, it is too easy for them to assume that you are one the 45% of Americans who will never attend college. If you are placed in classes where learning is not taking place, talk to your parents – they will not know there is a problem if you don't tell them. If your parents push for it, they can help move you into a more appropriate class, and help motivate teachers, not doing their jobs, to get back on track.

I was surprised when my son was having difficulty in a math class. Then I found out the most of the students in his class were earning D's or below. I took it up with his counselor – who did not believe the situation I described until I pushed hard enough for her to investigate. Teacher was changed the next day, and my son moved to a more advanced class. Teachers are typically observed and evaluated by school administrators for less than 15 minutes per year. If they are doing a poor job and no one reports it, the administration never knows, and nothing changes.

AP Classes

Advanced Placement (AP) classes are usually taught at a much higher level than are honors classes. They can be so tough that they are often graded on a curve so that most students can pass. AP classes are usually scored on a 5-point scale rather than the 4.0 for an A as in regular classes. Thus, an A in an AP class can help boost your weighted GPA. AP classes usually take a considerable amount of work and may consume many hours of out of class study time. They are taught at about college level.

AP tests given at the end of the school year are scored from one to five. Most public colleges give credit for AP scores of three or higher, with some giving two semesters of college credit for scores of 4 or 5, depending on the class. Policies vary among colleges. High school students may be able to earn a year of college credit taking AP classes, it they attend a state colleges, however, many highly selective private colleges, give little in any college credits for passing AP exams. Nevertheless, success in AP classes demonstrates college readiness and can thus increase a student's chances of attaining admission into top ranked schools.

One problem with AP classes is that the teacher is under pressure. At the end of the year, the students take a nationally standardized test in the subject area. If the students perform poorly, it makes the teacher look bad, they may be removed from teaching the class, suffer humiliation and loss of income. At the same time, the teacher is under great pressure to speed through high volumes of complex material, even if they see that the students are not comprehending it.

In recent years, high schools in some states are graded on how many students take AP classes. Thus, more students are encouraged to take these courses, even if they are not ready for them. Teachers are under increasing pressure; they have more unprepared students in their classrooms that they are trying to prepare for the standardized test. This means your AP class may be comprised of unhappy students and an unhappy teacher, and you may need to spend more time out of the classroom studying AP prep guides in order to pass the tests.

When you get to college and take physics or chemistry, there are no standardized tests to show your proficiency. You are graded solely on how well you do in the class. Most grades in college are A's and B's. Earning a B grade in a college calculus course is unlikely to keep you out of graduate school. I submit for your consideration that a high school AP course may be more difficult than the college course you would otherwise take a couple of years later, by which time you should be better prepared for the challenge.

It may seem that I am discouraging you from taking AP classes. I am cautioning you to limit them. I advise even great students to enjoy school and not overload themselves with AP classes that use up too much free time. One or two AP class per year is enough to show colleges that you are not afraid of work and ready for college-level thinking. If you take AP classes, take ones that you are prepared for. If you have already taken honors chemistry, AP chemistry should not be a leap. However, as a first chemistry course, you may be setting yourself up for, at best, a difficult year and at worst, for disaster.

AP arts, such as AP Studio Art 2-D Design Portfolio or AP Music Theory, may be great classes for you if you excel in these areas. They do take time and self-discipline (a good thing), but are less likely to be stressful for most students than those in math and science. They also are less impressive to colleges.

Many competitive, private colleges do not give college credit for AP classes or only give credits for "5's". What they do consider, however, are the grade on your transcript, and they like to see that the student has taken and done well in these more challenging classes.

Nationally, 40 to 50% of students taking the AP test get a one or two on the test; nearly half of all students do not score well enough on the AP test to earn a 3, the minimum to receive college credit. If you are not working at an A level in an AP class, you should question whether you are in reach of a passing test score.

Even if you do take an AP class, *you may be better off not taking the AP Tests.* Before signing up for the class, check the teacher's previous class results and use Wikipedia to check the national AP pass rate for the class you are interested in*. Follow the link to the individual class and scroll down to find the pass rates. If the teacher at your school has a pass rate that is significantly below the national average, you might want to avoid that AP class, or avoiding taking the year-end AP test. If you want to take an AP class during high school just to get an introduction to the topic or because you enjoy it, that is fine. You are not obligated to take the end of year AP exam.

A pass rates lower than the national average does not mean the teacher as inept. Guidance counselors often put students in AP classes that don't belong there. The problem may be even larger. The AP pass rate for sciences for students in Florida is about 15% lower than the national average. This does not mean that students and teachers are worse in Florida, but more likely results from the mix of Florida students placed in AP classes. In 2010 in Florida, 43.5% of high school students took at least one AP class, while the national average was 28.3%. Since only about 13% of high school students nationally are ready for college-level

---

* http://en.wikipedia.org/wiki/Advanced_Placement

work, only about a third of those placed in AP classes in Florida are ready, and this is reflected in their scores. In Maryland, 301 per thousand high school students earn a three or above on at least one AP exam, while only 33 per thousand students from Louisiana do[3]. If you attend a small high school, it may not be possible to provide AP classes to the six students who are actually ready; the choice for the school is to fill the class with students that are not ready, or not teach the course.

You are not required to take the AP tests just because you took the class. Conversely, you can take the test even if you do not take the AP class. If you are an exceptional student of English literature or language, you might study and take the AP Language and AP Literature exams at the end of your junior year even though you may not have the opportunity to take one of these classes until your senior year. If you are an artist or photographer, you can prepare a portfolio even if you are not enrolled in an AP art class. Talk to your high school counselor early in the school year if you are interested in trying this.

Students that pass three or more AP tests are eligible for an AP Scholar Award. This is not monetary awards, but is an accolade that can be proudly presented on your application, which may help attain admission into a choice university or win a scholarship. Passing four AP exams with an average score over 3.0 merits an AP Scholar Honors Award[†]. These awards are most helpful if you have taken or 3 or 4 AP classes before your senior year so that you can tout the award on your college applications.

Failing to achieve acceptable scores on AP tests, however, may be embarrassing. If you get a one or a two on an AP test, you can pay the AP College board $10 per college per test to withhold the AP test results, so that the colleges you apply to do not see the low scores. However, since AP scores are requested on the Common Application and most other college applications, and an

---

[†] http://www.collegeboard.com/student/testing/ap/scholarawards.html

oath of veracity is required (with threat of revocation of any degree earned), I don't see how poor scores can be hidden.

It may be a reasonable strategy, when you are not doing well in the class or practice tests, to avoid taking AP exams other than at the end of your senior year. AP scores taken at the end of the senior year of high school are usually not be included in college applications, which should have been submitted well before these tests are taken. Most students will have been already been accepted for admission before the senior year tests scores are available. Thus, there is less reason to avoid taking AP classes at the end of the senior year if the student lacks confidence that they will pass the tests.

Dual Enrollment

Dual enrollment classes can be better opportunities than AP class. Dual enrollment classes count for both high school and college credit, and are usually easier than AP classes. Here, the teacher sets the standard and is not externally evaluated by standardized tests students take at the end of the year. The grade is based on how well you perform compared to your classroom peers. There should be little surprise; if you are not doing well, this will be evident from your scores throughout the school year, so you can adjust your efforts. With the AP test, however, you have to wait until July to find out if you failed the national test. In most dual enrollment classes, most of the students that do their class work are expected to pass with an A or B. Like AP classes, dual-enrollment classes are usually graded on a 5-point scale for your high school GPA.

Dual enrollment classes may be taught at your school or a nearby community college. Don't be intimidated – those community college students are likely no smarter or better prepared than you. If there is a choice between doing a dual enrollment class or an AP class, the dual enrollment class is likely to be less stressful, and less likely to result in negative consequences. Elite colleges, however, do not consider dual enrollment as rigorous as they do AP classes, which provide a standardized score. These colleges also are usually unimpressed by weighted GPA's and prefer the unweighed GPA score.

Be a smart shopper for all your classes. Investigate the classes and teachers at your school in the spring prior to selecting classes for the next school year. Find out if the workload is excessive, if the teacher is pleasant or unreasonable, interesting or dull. For AP classes, find out what the AP exam pass rate has been for their students. If the teacher is teaching both the honors and AP section, the workload may be very similar for both classes, in which case it would be advantageous to take the AP section. Try to get placed in classes where teachers enjoy the experience. You too will have a better educational experience, are likely to learn more, and get better grades when the teacher enjoys the class. You may be much happier in an honors class, earning a 4.5 point A from a relaxed, pleasant teacher, than getting a hard-earned 5.0 point A and failed AP test from a stressed-out AP teacher.

Get to know, and try to charm your guidance counselor. Let them know your aspirations to learn and to attend a competitive college. If they like you, they can steer you to the best classes.

Doing your homework in selecting the best teachers available can help your GPA, save you time and prevent needless stress for an entire year. Ask around. Find out what each teacher expects and how they test, so that you can provide them the performance that earns great grades. Remember: your time is both valuable and limited. You have other activities you need to allocate time for.

Selective colleges look at the difficulty of the classes you take. Getting an A in AP Calculus BC is much more impressive than an A in business math. An A in AP Calculus is going to help to get into M.I.T. or other highly selective school. However, for many scholarships, and for many other colleges, an A in honors algebra or dual enrollment college algebra is just as good, and a much easier way to achieve an A.

Competing for Grades

The word *compete* comes from the Latin: *competere*: to seek together. It is a quest where pairs or sets of individuals strive to accomplish an agreed-upon goal. It is not about destroying or harming other individuals, but rather each striving to exceed the other. In competition, we push ourselves harder. In a race with a friend, we both try harder. Thus, our competitors make us better, and we help them achieve more, as well.

Education is not a battleground for grades. It is working together to achieve personal development and learning. It is not a place for malevolence, chicanery, or malice. Great teachers don't pit students against each other in battle, nor ration the number of A's that students in the classroom can achieve. Rather, they strive to have everyone achieve excellence.

Battles Lost

During your schooling, you will likely get some grades lower than you had hoped, and likely, some lower than you deserved. Receiving an 89.8 B from a vindictive teacher who refuses to round up can be extremely maddening. When the class is over, move on and put it behind you. Remember in these moments that you also received A's in classes that were gifts you didn't really earn.

Don't allow yourself the luxury of feeling defeated from a poor grade. Colleges don't demand perfection. Sure, an undefeated team will head to the championship, but so will many other teams that lost some games during the season. When you get a grade that is not as good as you had hoped, be honest in assessing what you might have done, if anything, which could have helped, and what you can do better the next time.

Senioritis

Senioritis is a pathological state, manifesting the comorbidity of short-timer syndrome with spring fever. The final stretch of high school is overloaded with excitement and events, making it nearly impossible to focus on mundane class work. Students are preparing for graduation, prom, parties, and performances, and realizing that life is about to give way to the future. Yet, they still need to maintain their GPA, even after receiving their letter of acceptance to Princeton. If their grades tank, they can lose the seat at the university where they had been accepted.

Consider taking a lighter load the last semester of high school. AP or dual enrollment students may consider taking single semester courses in the first semester of your senior year, and then taking some fun elective classes for the second semester to lighten their load. Several single semester AP courses may be offered at your school: Psychology, U.S. Government and Politics, Microeconomics, and Macroeconomics. Many dual enrollment courses are also single semester classes. You also may prefer a shortened day for your last semester of high school to give more time to make preparations and enjoy yourself.

Summary

Take classes you are prepared for and that you can excel in and enjoy. The goal of education is to gain mastery of the subject, not to get a document saying that you passed or received an A. Taking one step at a time to build a sure foundation is far superior to jumping ahead and hoping that your leap gets you across the gaps in your knowledge. If you make a habit of leaping chasms, you will eventually fall into a pit.

Time invested preparing for college placement tests will return more benefit than time spent struggling through AP classes in hopes of avoiding a college course later on. Honors classes and dual-enrollment are sweet spots in education. Take advantage of these classes when possible.

If you run into trouble in a class, ask for help. Get a tutor. With the help of someone who has a clear understanding of the material, it may take a few minutes to figure out something you otherwise would struggle with for hours, and still not get right.

Using a personal organizer, a calendar, and organizing your papers take little intelligence but can help boost your grades and help make you look brilliant. Neat handwriting and organized work allow teachers to easily recognize your understanding of the material and help you earn extra points.

Plan ahead in the first years of high school so that you will have enough credits that you can have a lightened load or shortened school day for your last semester of high school.

Work smarter, not harder!

Once you get all A's, you can never go back. A 4.0 is addicting.
~Mikael Genai

Cynicism is the flawed logic of a person who has chosen to neglect their role as a force for change in this world.
~Unknown

Chapter 5: Letters of Recommendation

If you have knowledge, let others light their candles in it.

~Margaret Fuller

Job interviews are used by employers to select individuals that they believe will earn more money for the company than the employee costs, who will make the company a better place to work, and who will improve the reputation of the company.

Colleges have similar goals. Letters of recommendation are used to determine if you are likely to benefit the college. Students benefit the university when they bring intellectual diversity and creative thinking, make the university a better environment for learning, contribute to research efforts, and improve the university's reputation through their future successes. When they accept a student, they are making an investment.

Colleges are looking for creative, amiable individuals, with high integrity and alacrity for learning. Letters of recommendation can evince these things about you and may bring across strengths not be revealed other places in your application.

Focus extra energy in a few classes where you can shine like the brightest star. For some colleges, and for many scholarships, you will need letters of recommendation. The Common App requests two, preferably from teachers from your junior or senior year.

Try to cultivate relationships with at least three teachers who will write outstanding recommendations for you. You will need to earn the respect of these teachers, so much so that they feel personally invested in your future. Find a few classes where you excel and make sure that you impress those teachers. Be polite. Control any urge to display arrogance with your teachers. Earn their respect by going beyond the assigned workload required to get an A to excel in these classes, so that you stand out from other students. Be a leader in the class. You want a "best student it has been my pleasure to teach" letter of recommendation from these teachers. There is no benefit from having a dozen "She (he) did their assignments well and got an A in my class" letters. You want three letters that show that the teacher considered you exceptional, even if it means you apply less effort in some other classes as a result. Nevertheless, do not allow other classes to suffer to the point that they fall below the 2.5% rule. Colleges usually prefer letters from the student's junior year, so this is the time to shine.

A Science, a Humanities and an Elective

At least one outstanding performance should be in a science class. Science classes often have projects that give an opportunity to shine. An English or history class is another area where you can go beyond the expected by taking extra effort to produce high-quality assignments beyond the expected A level work. Another area to excel in is an elective, such as art, music, service-learning or in an extracurricular or work activity. Outstanding recommendations from three different areas will present a much stronger commendation and be more attractive to a college or university than if the recommendations come from a single area of strength for an individual. You don't want to look like a kid who is wizard in one area but mediocre in most. It's better to excel in many areas.

Helping tutor other kids in the classroom or being a leader in discussions that keep the class interesting and help to keep the class focused and on topic can gain you respect from the teacher. You want to give the teacher material so that they can tell their personal story about how you made a positive difference in their life or the life of other students in their class.

Quietly doing your work and getting an A will not suffice. To get positive accolades from a teacher, you need to actively participate in the class, show interest, do extra reading, and ask stimulating questions that help everyone in the class get the point of the lesson. This helps the teacher teach more effectively.

On the flip side, descriptions of how hard you work are not what you want in the letter of recommendation. You want letters from teachers for classes that have truly interested and inspired you. You want to be seen as a natural; where the class was easy for you. You never want a letter relating that you had to use maximal effort to get an A. Even worse is if you grubbed for that A, or had to do make-up or extra credit work to get it. There are times when you may need to do that extra credit work, but that is not a teacher you want to ask for a letter of recommendation.

Effective letters of recommendation get to the point. Unless your grades in the first two years of high school were terrible, you do not want a letter saying that you turned your life around. Imagine a letter for a student that begins:

> *"When I first met Jill she had just rolled down the hill and into the back of my classroom in a wheelchair. Her jaw was wired shut, and she was on medications, so she often fell asleep in class. Later, her mother was in prison, and she spent time living in an abandoned warehouse. She had miserable self-esteem and participated little in the classroom."*

Even though the letter goes on to describe how Jill went on to be valedictorian, and did things that showed tremendous strength, courage, dedication and intelligence, a reviewer may already have the picture of someone unlikely to contribute to the intellectual environment of the university.

A letter for the same person might begin:

"Jill is a student of tremendous strength, courage, dedication and intelligence. She has been an inspiration to all of us, earned the respect and admiration of her peers, and thus, was chosen to be her class's valedictorian. It is not just what she has achieved so much as the grace and generosity she has shown while accomplishing it."

If you ever weed a garden, you know it is easy to pull out the flowers and vegetables along with the weeds if you are not paying attention. Remember that the reviewer is reading dozens of letters and may be tired, hungry, and speeding through stacks of applications. The reviewer is likely to make snap judgments, and to look for reasons, even when not well founded, to weed out what may appear to be weaker candidates.

Think of the letters of recommendation as an executive summary designed to make it easy for the reviewer to see the salient points.

"Julian is the most creative and cerebral writer in my AP Composition and Language class. His participation in class discussions has raised the level of dialog and interest."

The story of a student progressing from ordinary skill to extraordinary talent should be celebrated. However, one which tells of your progression from weakness or failure; how quiet or distracted your were, or even how hard working you are, should be avoided. The person writing your letter of recommendation may be happy to rewrite to make it more effective. If they have discussed prior weaknesses, don't be afraid to politely ask if they would simply say why you are a great candidate *now*.

If your inglorious past is highlighted in the introduction to the letter of recommendation, you might say, "I'm not that person anymore. I would rather not be remembered in that way." The teacher has already given you their endorsement; you are unlikely to lose it asking for a simpler letter.

Unfortunately, you will likely never see your letters of recommendation, and thus, may not be able to comment. If you think your teacher is likely to write a turn-around letter, you can let them read this chapter.

The School Report

The Common App requires a report from your counselor, in which they are asked to evaluate you with the option of writing a letter. *They will not be able to help you much if they don't know you and like you.* Many competitive colleges will call to interview the high school councilors of top candidates. Get to know your counselor. Make sure that they are aware of your extracurricular and community service activities, your aspirations, and your desire to attend a great college. At the beginning of your senior year, give them a copy of your C.V. (Chapter 15). They may help improve it, and at the same time, they can learn more about you.

If your counselor does not know you (or if you feel they won't write a helpful letter), you can ask to have another school official who knows you better write the letter for the school report.

The Common App asks teachers to rate students on a 1 – 5 scale in several different areas, such as contribution to class discussion, classroom behavior and intellectual prowess. They are also given a chance to provide a narrative assessment.

NOTE: Some colleges do not request letters of recommendation, and others do not weigh them heavily in the application process. They are, however, often used in making competitive scholarship decisions.

Use what talents you possess; the woods would be very silent if no birds sang there except those that sang best.

~Henry Van Dyke

Chapter 6: Scoring Higher on Placement Tests

Whether you think you can or think you can't – you are right.

~Henry Ford

Consider the amount of time you dedicate to homework in a year. Perhaps better put, how many hours of work would it take you to earn A's in all of your classes? If you go to a demanding prep school, you may have 3 or more hours of homework each night for about 180 days a year, plus work on weekends and required summer reading. Now, add the hours of class work. Multiply that for four years of school. These comprise the thousands of hours of work performed to earning the GPA upon which colleges judge you.

Scoring high on the ACT or SAT is at least as important for in gaining admission to a competitive school as is a transcript replete with A's. Superior grades are required for admission into competitive schools. Great ACT or SAT scores are also essential. A student with less than perfect grades, but with exceptional prep test scores, looks brilliant. A college may assume the student had uninspiring classes, was bored, or involved in other activities, yet has great intellectual potential. If you want to make this case, you will need to provide evidence of it.

Earning great ACT or SAT scores takes much less work than a heavy load of AP classes. An AP test can be repeated the following year, if a poor score is earned, but few students ever bother. If you are disappointed by your score on a college placement test, for about $50, you can take it again. Most students repeat the ACT or SAT tests in an attempt to earn a higher score. AP Biology, AP Calculus, and AP Physics will not prepare you to take the ACT or SAT much better than honors algebra. Time and effort spent preparing for the ACT will yield more benefit in getting into an elite college than time used on a crushing AP class load.

If you weighed the impact of college placement tests on gaining acceptance into competitive colleges, it would justify spending a third of your high school educational efforts in preparation for these tests. *On a value basis, these tests are more important than an entire year of high school academic work.*

Consider then that most students spend only a few hours preparing for the ACT and SAT tests; mainly cramming for a few days or even just the night before the test. The time required to prepare adequately for these tests is far more than a student can set aside in a few weeks leading up to the tests. Students should begin preparing for placement tests in the freshman or sophomore year of high school.

Why spend the time? *Preparation for these tests may be the highest returning investment you ever make.* Even if you can glide into the state college of your choice with a mediocre score, it may still be worth the effort to get a great score. It makes it much easier to get scholarships or have your tuition paid for you. Even if the school you want to get into accepts students with midrange ACT scores (about 22), they are likely to recruit students with a 30 or better by offering scholarships. A score in the top three percent, along with good grades, earns many students a free ride; free tuition and housing, at a selective private college.

In many ways, college placement tests tell as much about the time and planning a student put into preparation as it reveals about their intellectual aptitude. This is not such a bad thing.

Students with above-average intelligence, who can focus, and are willing to invest time in their education can get excellent ACT and SAT scores. These are likely the same students who do well in universities that are more competitive. Having a very high IQ can also sometimes get a student a high score all by itself, but that high IQ is neither a requirement nor a guarantee of success on these tests.

What do placement tests actually test?

- Intelligence Quotient (IQ), especially the SAT
- Acquired knowledge
- Quality of education
- Self-discipline
- Drive (including how hard your mama drives you)
- Test anxiety (a negative)
- Social-economic status
- Maturity
- Preparation
- Courage and self-confidence

Preparation may be more important than exceptional intelligence. In 1997, only 74 students earned a perfect 36 on the ACT. By 2011, 704 students did so, but the number of students taking the test had less than doubled. The perfect score rate increased by more than five times over 14 years. It is unlikely that the native intelligence of students rose much in 14 years. These high scores have increased because more students prepare, and more people have figured out how to prepare effectively. Once you know how, great scores are not out of reach.

Prep books: There are many prep books for the SAT and ACT. Barron's tends to be more difficult, Princeton Review the most popular. Others use different types of questions that approximate the test. However, there is a more effective strategy.

The tests need to remain very similar year to year to get reliable results. Colleges rely on the ACT; a score of 27 in the year 2017 needs to ranks student's academic prowess the same as it did in 2003. To make the test valid, similar questions are used that test the same areas of knowledge at the same level of difficulty.

The test questions need to change, however, or it would be easy to learn the test. Thus, the College Board, which creates the SAT, uses very similar questions year to year. The ACT test does the same. These questions and their level of difficulty have been tested on millions of students over the years. These companies are experts in creating questions that reliably assess the level of the material tested. From test to test, the format remains the same with the same number and type of questions. If you learn how to approach and answer questions on an old test, you should be able to answer analogous questions when you take the placement test.

Thus, the best study material to practice is with the actual ACT or SAT tests. Studying the questions from retired tests will prepare you for answering new questions on new tests. Algebra, logic, and correct use of language have not changed in the last 60 years, and neither has the knowledge base needed for these tests.

Retired ACT and SAT tests are available from the companies who make the actual tests. They are published as books: "Real ACT Prep Guide" published by Peterson's and "The Official SAT Study Guide" published by the College Board.

The same strategy can be used for the MCAT, LSAT, and GRE for medical, law and graduate school. Purchase the guide published by the testing company. They will have the test questions that best prepare you for the actual test. They often explain why the wrong answer is wrong, which is just as important as why the correct answer is right.

Usually, there is little need to worry about getting the newest edition. These books change very little most years, and the brand new edition typically has nothing new. New editions are published each year, as the publisher needs to keep an income stream, but typically, little inside the book has changed.

In 2011 *Real ACT Prep Guide* 3rd edition was expanded from having three tests to five retired tests. These tests are the reason to buy the book, so find a recent one. Most people do not find the

CD to be of any benefit, so you can save a few dollars and get the book without the CD.

Another CD does have value. It is <u>Boost Your Score! The Unofficial Software Guide to the Real ACT</u> disk. This program allows you to enter your test results from the five tests in the *Real ACT Prep Guide*, plus one downloadable ACT practice test. The program then gives you scores on various areas within the test. It shows you your weak areas and gives you links to study material to help remedy these deficiencies. Additionally, it provides some simple math programs for TI calculators that can be used during the ACT test to help save time.

A free, limited version of the software can be downloaded so that you can try it with a free, official ACT practice test also available online. The free version of the Boost program can be downloaded at http://whatsyouradvantage.org/boost-lite/.

An ACT practice test booklet may be available in your school's guidance office. If not, it is also available for download at: http://media.actstudent.org/documents/preparing.pdf. The ACT changes the practice tests in their booklets every three years. They have published four different practice tests since 2003. These tests are available for download at this book's website at https://sites.google.com/site/collegeprepguidebook/. The password, required for some supplemental materials, is given on the first page of Appendix A of this book. Thus, four practice from the ACT tests can be downloaded free of cost, in addition to the five retired tests available in the *Real ACT Prep Guide*.

For the SAT, *The Official SAT Study Guide* 2nd edition contains ten retired tests. You may also find a sample SAT test in your high school's guidance office.

TAKE NOTE: In March of 2016 the SAT will introduce a new test that has major changes in its format. Older SAT study materials may not be helpful for preparing for the new test.

The material on the ACT, SAT and even on the GRE used for admission to graduate school, is not advanced mathematics, science, linguistics, or literature. These tests are designed to assess fundamentals. The knowledge base required to attain great scores is taught mostly in the eighth and ninth grades. Nonetheless, ascendancy on the ACT requires mastery of these fundamentals. If grammar, 8th-grade math, algebra, and geometry are somewhat foggy concepts; you will need to work on them until they are crystal clear to achieve a superior ACT score.

SAT or ACT

The SAT remains more popular for colleges in the heartland of the country. Meanwhile, colleges along the East and West Coasts prefer the ACT. In the past, I recommended concentrating on one test, and usually, the ACT, as it was easier to prepare for, especially when time was limited.

With the new SAT, however, I recommend preparing and taking both. Most colleges accept either one, and studying for either one will help raise scores on the other. Different people perform differently on these tests; you may not know until you try which you will be stronger on. Preparing for both tests is like cross-training as an athlete; each will help you develop different academic strengths and skills.

Some students perform better on the SAT. The ACT is a speed test. If you are a student with superior language skills, but finish tests more slowly than most of your classmates, the SAT may be for you. SAT questions are more cognitively complex; however, it allows more time per question than does the ACT. If time limits are your greatest foil on tests, consider the SAT.

The SAT will be modernized in 2016 to better align with newer concepts in education. The new emphasis will be on evidence – based reading and writing. There will be less emphasis on arcane vocabulary but more on language use. There will be less emphasis on computation, but more on how to approach real-world math problems.

These changes seem appropriate. Much of our work uses computers; they are great at computation and can help fix grammar. It makes sense for the SAT to test the skills we need in life that computers do not do for us. The College Board is also changing the SAT for economic reasons; the new test will likely be used, as the ACT is in many states, as a standardized high school competency test required for graduation.

The PSAT is usually given in the sophomore year. High PSAT score can provide high achieving students eligibility for the National Merit Scholarships. Students astute enough to begin preparation for placement tests early in high school can use SAT prep materials to preparation for the PSAT, and get a step ahead on preparation for the SAT and ACT. The PSAT will also be updated, beginning in October of 2015.

Differences between the ACT and SAT:

1. ACT questions tend to be more straightforward, using simpler English language construction than the SAT.
2. The SAT has a stronger emphasis on abstruse vocabulary, although they are changing their emphasis in this area.
3. The ACT has a science section, which is just more critical reading. The SAT does not have a science section.
4. The SAT has more sections and is a longer test: the ACT is 2 hours 55 minutes (without the 30-minute writing test, and the SAT is 3 hours 45 minutes. The New SAT will be three hours, and the essay section will be 50 minutes.
5. The SAT is more about problem solving, while the ACT evaluates more what has been learned.
6. Both tests have grammar questions. The ACT asks more questions about punctuation. The new SAT will ask more about ideas.

7. On the SAT, the questions get more difficult as the test progresses, but they are not progressive on the ACT.
8. There is not penalty for wrong answers on the ACT or the new SAT, but there is a small penalty on the current SAT.
9. The ACT has four (three simple and one more difficult) trig questions. Otherwise, the level of math difficulty is similar on both tests. (See Appendix B for trig tips.) The new SAT will emphasize problem-solving.
10. A perfect score on the SAT is 800, and 500 is average. A perfect score on the ACT is 36, and 21 to 22 is average.
11. Your SAT essay may be seen by to colleges you apply to (So be nice!). The new SAT essay will require reading and a factual analysis of a source document.
12. The new SAT will have four rather than five answers to multiple choice questions

The old SAT was designed to test aptitude. The ACT tests achievement. It is more difficult to augment aptitude than to learn the material covered in the ACT. The old SAT favors students who have benefited from better educational environments; those of higher socio-economic status; those who have done more reading, especially of classical literature; and those with better verbal skills. It relies more on complex vocabulary and concepts, making it harder for students that have not had a top-notch education. Raising SAT scores requires more preparation time than does the ACT, as the SAT requires not only learning subject matter and vocabulary, but also learning to use language and think complexly.

The new SAT will likely continue to favor those privileged with a higher quality education. This is what you want; an education that prepares you to understand and use information from your world so that you can do the things you want to do. But not everyone gets a quality education. If you have taken AP language, it should help prepare you for the new SAT. Taking science classes that require the use of math to solve problems also helps. The new SAT demands critical thinking and multistep problem-solving. The emphasis will not be so much on how much you know, but more on how well you use a core knowledge base. It will test mastery of the concepts you have learned in school. The new SAT will be a better test, and one, which you will be able to train for.

The ACT tests materials taught in school more directly, and preparing for it is more straightforward. The downside of the ACT is that it is a speed test. Cautious students, who take more time to work problems, will not score as well. The SAT allows enough time for most students, but asks questions obliquely, making it more difficult to figure out what is being asked.

The Appendices at the end of this book contain material, tips, and traps that are useful in preparing for both tests.

How to use Test Prep Materials:

To earn a superior score on the ACT or SAT, start preparing for the test several months or more prior to taking the test. Read the instructions in the practice booklets to learn about the test, its rules, and which subject materials are covered in the tests.

Begin by printing the answer sheets (Pages 73 through 78 from the online ACT practice tests) to use when doing the practice tests. (Each ACT practice document is 80 pages.) These answer sheets can also be used for the test that is in the *Real ACT Prep Guide* and will allow you to work on better quality paper than the newsprint used for the book.

Begin studying for the test by taking a baseline practice test; for the ACT, use either the online example or one from the book, which you can score with the *Boost Your Score!* program. Don't worry if it takes far more time than allotted to take your first practice tests. Later, after you have learned more content, you will be able to take the test more quickly.

Work your way through the practice test and then score it with the *Boost Your Score* program. This will act as a diagnostic and help you understand where you need to focus your learning. If you don't know how to approach a problem, or you are guessing – leave it blank. The goal for this first test is to diagnose your weak areas. If you happen to guess correctly, you will lose the chance to learn something you need to know.

Later, go over the questions that you either got wrong or left blank, and learn to solve these problems. This may take a couple of weeks, working an hour a day. The goal is to fill in the blanks in knowledge so that you will be able to get these questions right the next time. These are fill-in-the-blank tests. It is essential to understand why you answered incorrectly to enable you to fill in the blanks in your knowledge.

Check the answer section in the book for the questions you get wrong, and figure out *why* you got it wrong. If you are making careless mistakes or filling in the wrong circle, focus on more care in this area. These are points easy to fix. If you didn't know how to answer, make sure you use sources that teach you to understand the material so that you can get the questions right the next time you have similar material in a question.

Next, after the first practice test, use the *Real ACT Prep Guide* or downloadable ACT practice tests for studying. Go over each question carefully to learn the subject matter you need to answer each question correctly. Do at least three more tests as open book tests, taking as much time as you need to work the problems and learn how to answer those questions you don't know. The goal is to learn what you don't know, as well as to learn how to approach reading the questions.

If you don't know grammar rules, it's time to learn them. A brief grammar summary is provided in Appendix C at the end of this book, and strategies for the reading section are provided in Appendix D. For math questions, try to solve the problems using the brute force method, but also learn how to solve them quickly. Brute force usually works but takes more time. Brute force refers to trying out each answer to see which of the five works. Appendix B at the end of this book gives some math tips, traps, and trigonometry help for college placement tests.

If you start practicing with tests in your sophomore year or earlier, you will have plenty of time to learn how to quickly solve the problems. In the language sections, learn how to answer each question correctly. It does not matter if it takes an hour every evening for a few weeks to work through a single test that you will later have to complete in only a couple of hours. The goal is to learn how to approach answering every question correctly. This is the route to a high score. Guessing is a strategy for earning a low score. *No guessing is allowed!*

Hard Questions: Many of the questions look much harder than they are. Most math questions require only simple algebra or basic geometry. Keep in mind that the test is as much a test of your calm as of your brilliance. They contain difficult-appearing problems that intimidate many students, causing them to skip over them, even when the questions are not actually difficult. Often if a question looks hard, you are looking at it wrong. Remember, especially on the SAT, the answer may require multiple logical steps to get the answer.

When you work through the test, and you get an incorrect answer, do a diagnostic. Why did you get it wrong if you were not guessing? Some of the answers are trick answers. In these questions, try to understand why each wrong answer is wrong, as well as why the right answer is right. On the SAT, questions become progressively more difficult as the test goes on; questions that appear easy in the later part of the SAT may be tricky. On the new SAT, however, they have promised to get rid of "trick" questions, designed to throw people off course with superficially obvious questions.

Real-Time Practice: After working through several practice tests, begin practicing time-limited testing. Do at least three time-limited practice tests in preparation for taking the actual test. If you want to run quarter mile sprints – practice sprints. If you want to swim the English Channel, running sprints as practice will not hurt but does little to prepare you for the challenge. These tests are endurance tests. This is especially true of the new SAT, as is demands three hours of nearly continuous critical thinking and problem solving. Most of it is not hard, but it demands focused attention for three hours, and nearly four with the "optional" essay, that most colleges request.

When writing the SAT essay, keep in mind that they send a copy of your SAT essay to the colleges you apply to. I don't if anyone ever looks at them, but just in case, try not to write anything that would embarrass you.

Perform the tests as if you were doing the real thing, with the exception that you should make a mark on the sheet for any answer that you were unsure of or guessing at. Similarly, if you plan to use a calculator, use it on at least three practice tests. BTW, use of calculators will not be permitted for 20 of the 57 math questions on the new SAT.

Go to bed early on Friday night, get up at 7:00 A.M. on Saturday morning, have your breakfast, and at 8:00 A.M. do a complete test, taking a 15-minute break between sections.

Later go back, score yourself, and do a diagnostic. Go back to any question you got wrong and any that you marked as being unsure of. These are your weak areas, even if you guessed correctly. Learn how to do these questions. This is the most important thing you can do: overcome your weak areas. If you how to answer a question, learn how. Keep a notebook or 3x5 inch index cards with the grammar rules or math tips you are adding to your cognitive toolbox, so that you can review them.

If you purchased the *Boost Your Score* program, use it and look at the guides they provide. If you do not understand the test material, ask a teacher or tutor at your school for help. Remember, most of the content on these test is not difficult, but you need to understand it well. If you do not comprehend it, you may be making it more difficult than it is.

Sometimes, you may miss a question even when you know the right answer. You may have transcribed your answer to the wrong space, or misplaced a decimal. These little errors are common on the actual tests, and learning to avoid them can make a large difference in your score. This may be the easiest area to pick up points. Learn why you made the mistake and figure out methods to prevent similar errors that are easily avoided.

Registry errors occur on these tests when the test taker fills in the wrong line of bubbles. Don't leave blanks. When bubbles are empty, or if questions are approached out of order, it is easy to fill in the wrong bubble. If the test taker accidentally fills a bubble in the wrong place, every answer down the column that follows may be entered into the wrong space. Check frequently to ensure that answers are placed in the correctly numbered space on the answer sheet. Additionally, always mark your answer in the question booklet; if you need to go back and fix this type of error, you can do it quickly.

Never guess on practice tests: If you guess correctly on practice questions, you will not be able to diagnose where you need to focus your learning. The purpose of the practice is to learn how to approach and understand the questions. If you don't know the answer a question on practice test mark the bubble for your best guess with an x or other mark to distinguish it, and score these separately – to see how well you are guessing. Later go back and learn how to answer these questions.

Always guess on the real tests: On the old SAT, scoring is balanced so that blind guessing does not help nor hurt. In a question with five answers, a point is earned for the correct answer, and ¼ of a point is lost for a wrong answer. Do the math: 1 – (4 x ¼) = 0. If you have an inkling, or can eliminate even one wrong answer, you have raised the odds of earning points. The ACT, new SAT, and AP tests do not have a penalties" for wrong answers. Guessing can allow more time to focus on questions you know how to approach.

If you are unsure of an answer, go ahead and fill in your best guess on the answer sheet, but make a note in the test booklet, such as drawing a circle around the question so that if you have time, you can go back and easily find it, and give it more thought. If you are completely clueless, fill in a bubble to lower the risk of making registration errors from having empty spaces.

If all but one answer appear correct, read the question more carefully. In math, there is only one right answer. In other areas, read all the answers; there is sometimes more than one correct answer. Your job is to find the best answer.

Reading: You can expect to increase your proficiency at answering math and grammar questions quickly as you practice and learn the material and how to approach different types of questions. In the reading and science sections of the ACT, however, time becomes a critical barrier. Many students run out of time and are unable to complete these sections. Appendix D gives strategies for approaching the reading sections and on managing and optimizing the limited time available.

On the SAT (but not the ACT), the questions are generally presented in the same order as the material in the. The first questions will ask about things early in the passage, and later questions about things farther on. Knowing this will allow you to search for answers more efficiently, and focus on what is asked in the questions. When practicing the critical reading and science tests, try reading the questions (but not the answers) before reading the passages to see if this helps you. You may find it helpful to underline the area in the passage relating to the questions as you read. As you practice taking the tests, you can refine those strategies that work best for you.

The new SAT will still require mastery of vocabulary; however, the emphasis will change from knowing definitions of obscure words to understanding and using "Tier Two" words. These are words common in college-level work. Some Tier Two words are specific, and have fairly narrow use, such as "synthesis" or "isotope." The SAT, however, will focus on Tier Two words that have different meanings depending on their context within a sentence or paragraph.

The word "radical" may refer to an extremist or to an atom with an unpaired electron. It may mean comprehensive as in surgery, refer to a root; such as a cube root in math, or a shoot growing from a root of a plant. The word "sanction" can mean punishment, to penalize, to boycott, or it can mean to authorize or support. It can be a noun or a verb. The new SAT will ask what a word means within the context of the sentence.

The appendices at the end of this book have material to help prepare for college placement tests. Grammar and punctuation are an easy area to pick up points on these tests. You may need to peruse these appendices several times to master them.

Ineffective Readers: Even very bright individuals may be ineffective readers. They may be slow readers, may space-out while reading, or may have difficulty understanding text that they just read – even when they read aloud fluently. A young man I know graduated second in his class, but when he enrolled in community college, he was unable to do his work. When I tested him, he read on a second-grade level. He could read any word on a page, read and answer brief test questions, but could not tell what he had just read if it was more than two lines of text.

Ineffective readers tend to read one word at a time, lose their place in the paragraph, or reread the same words the same words over. (Confusing, isn't it?) A lack of confidence or lack of understanding can promote rereading. Sometimes, an entire sentence must be read to get the meaning. Less confident readers may get confused half-way through longer sentences that don't make sense part way through or with poorly written sentences.

Many students, especially ineffective readers, can benefit from "speed reading" software, which trains the eyes and brain to coordinate better, avoid rereading text, and read by "phrases of meaning." This increases reading speed and comprehension. The goal should be to read with high comprehension at 210 to 250 words a minute. Anyone taking the placement tests may benefit from practicing reading at the ideal range for the reading sections of the placement tests. Use these programs to practice reading larger chunks of words at a time and to build confidence that helps avoid rereading words and phrases. Focus on visualizing phrases when reading. Ignore the hype about training to reading over 600 words a minute or to eliminating subvocalization.

Some highly rated programs include 7 Speed Reading, Readers Edge, and AceReader Pro. A free, online speed-reading program is available at www.readspeeder.com, and www.acereader.com has a free demo program.

Do your trial runs at home; not at the test center. Many students take the ACT or SAT just to see how they will do. Avoid this. Even though you can repeat these tests, colleges will see all your scores. Register for tests at least two months ahead of the date you want to take it to make sure you get a seat and to avoid late registration fees. Students from low-income families can take advantage of fee waivers for these tests from their high school counselor (one time for each for the ACT and SAT tests).

The strategic time to take college placement tests is when you are best prepared, but early enough to have results for your college selection and applications. June tests, before your senior year are the last ones that give scores in time for early admission applications. If you want two shots at the test, take one earlier in the second semester of your junior year, and reserve June as a backup for a redo. Taking AP language is excellent preparation for these tests. Most students are less distracted in the early months of the year; January through March of your junior year is often the best time to achieve high scores on these tests.

The deadline for registration is about five weeks before the tests, and some testing sites run out of available seats. Sign up early. The ACT is given in February, April, and June, and the SAT is offered in January, March, May, and June. Both are also given in the fall.

In the days before the test: Review the test rules, so that you don't waste time reading during the test or bring prohibited materials. Make sure your calculator is a permitted model and has fresh batteries. Do not take a cell phone or other prohibited items. Make sure that you have enough (3) pencils with erasers.

Try to get at least nine hours of sleep every night for the week prior to the test to eliminate any sleep deficit you many have. Since the tests are on a Saturdays during the school year, you should be accustomed to getting up and being awake at 7:00 A.M. If not, get your sleep cycle in gear several days before the test so that you will be alert and at your best. The night before the test, have a nice dinner, watch a comedy, relax. Get to bed early, by ten P.M. at the latest. You want to wake up refreshed. Last minute cramming only adds stress and fatigues your brain.

Caffeinated beverages may help get you going, but too much caffeine will make you feel jittery and nervous. If you want to use coffee or other caffeinated beverage to get your brain going the morning of the test, make sure that you have tested its effects on you in the same quantity on a practice test morning.

If you are interested in doing a placement test preparation course on-line or in a practice center, get started by the summer before your junior year. It takes time, time you may not have during a busy school year.

Theanine, an amino acid found in black tea, is calming. In combination with the caffeine in tea, theanine can improve reaction time and mental performance[4]. Tea, made from *one* bag of regular black tea plus one of decaf black tea can boost alertness with less risk of jitters and scattered attention than with other caffeinated beverages. More caffeine does not improve performance. High doses of caffeine can even slow the brain.

Having a snack and a beverage during test breaks can recharge your brain. Prepare them the day before the test so that you can take them with you. Take some change along for the vending machine in case the test center does not allow your snack inside.

Make sure you know the building at which the test is given, and how to get there. Tests are often given on college campuses that may be more than a mile across and in buildings far from easy parking. If you have not been there before, look on a map to see how to get to the building. It is a good idea to actually go to the building on a day prior to the test, to make sure you know how to get there, how long it may take, and where you can park or be dropped off. You don't want to find out on the morning of the test that one-way streets, lack of parking, or traffic barriers, which are common on college campuses, keep you from getting to the test on time. Although a mad dash running across campus in the cool morning air may get the blood running through your brain, being on time and calm is more conducive to success than a tense freak-out where you are screaming at your mom about being late.

TIP: Do "Victory Dance" (Chapter 14) just before tests.

To achieve greatness, start where you are, use what you have, do what you can.
                                                        ~Arthur Ashe

Chapter 7: Gaming the ACT Writing Section

The thing that is really hard, and really amazing, is giving up on being perfect and beginning the work of becoming yourself.

~Anna Quindlen

The college entrance exams are designed to measure intelligence, aptitude, knowledge, and math and language skills. These are all handy abilities to have, and I recommend using the time spent in high school to develop them. They are helpful not only for use on college placement tests, but also throughout your academic life and in your career.

In the new SAT test, students will read a short article, and have 55 minutes to write a fact-based analysis about it. Since the test is new, we can withhold judgment, and hope that scores will reflect the cognitive and literary ability of test taker. The ACT writing section, however, is not a test of creativity, intelligence, literary skill, knowledge, or even of how well you communicate on paper.

College students or schoolteachers score the writing tests using a standardized metric so that scoring will be consistent for the millions of students taking the tests. The metric does not score for knowledge. It does not care if you have brilliantly resolved a major social issue with your unrivaled sophistry. It does not award points for humor, hooks, clever ideas, or language, even though these are essential to good writing.

The graders are trained to evaluate the essays by a standardized protocol that does not consider these attributes. They do not give points for a concise, well thought-out essay. They are not sticklers on spelling or punctuation. Use of a cultivated vocabulary provides limited benefit. They do not fact-check your arguments or sources. You can make completely bogus arguments based on fantasized quotations from your Navy Seal, Native-American aunt that fought in Afghanistan, who doesn't exist. You will achieve just as good a score with material invented as you write as if you memorized and quoted from scholarly academic sources.

Here are the ACT test book guidelines for a perfect score of six:

"The essay shows a clear understanding of the task. The essay takes a position on the issue and may offer a critical context for discussion. The essay addresses complexity by examining different perspectives on the issue, or by evaluating the implications and/or complications of the issue, or by fully responding to counter-arguments to the writer's position. Development of ideas is ample, specific, and logical. Most ideas are fully elaborated. A clear focus on the specific issue in the prompt is maintained. The organization of the essay is clear: the organization may be somewhat predictable, or it may grow from the writer's purpose. Ideas are logically sequenced. Most transitions reflect the writer's logic and are usually integrated into the essay. The introduction and conclusion are effective, clear, and well developed. The essay shows a good command of language. Sentences are varied and word choice is varied and precise. There are few, if any, errors to distract the reader."

This sounds like a complex task, not only for the writer, but also for the person performing the scoring. How do the test graders tell if an essay has met these goals? Remember, the scorers are mostly college kids earning extra cash. Some aspects of these criteria are easy to grade, some are not. Criteria that are simple to grade get graded. They are also aspects that are easy to comply with when writing.

1. *Development of ideas is ample. Most ideas are fully elaborated.*

Put yourself in the grader's shoes. Which item is easiest to grade? *Ample* means sizable; thus, make it long. *The most important factor determining the essay's score is the length of the essay.*

Just in case you missed it: The number-one component that determines your score, is how long your essay is. The test gives you four pages for the ACT. Plan to write at least 3½ pages for the ACT to earn a high score. You want a long essay, but you don't have much time. You need to be verbose. Do not try using oversized letters or skipping lines. It will not fool them. Use a normal-sized handwriting and make it legible. Do not skip lines between paragraphs, but be sure to indent to make it clear where a new paragraph begins. Make sure you essay is long!

2. *The organization of the essay is clear: the organization may be somewhat predictable, or it may grow from the writer's purpose. Ideas are logically sequenced.*

Organization: Other easily gradable traits include having a coherent organization a clear thesis, and logical sequence; and ample elaboration of the ideas.

Make it easy for the grader to see that you complied with the "logically sequenced" criteria. This can be most transparently accomplished by conforming to the elementary 1:3:1 format that you were taught in the 5th grade. Include an introductory argument with three points; three expository paragraphs; one for each point, and a concluding paragraph. Tell them what you're going to tell them, tell them, tell them what you told them. Outline – expand – summarize. If you find this format boring, trite, juvenile, and pedantic, remember, *predictable* gets points and this is a test not of your writing skills or wit, but rather of your ability to conform to the metric used to score this test.

The test booklet gives blank pages to organize your thoughts. Take two or three minutes to outline what you want to say, and then get going. Work quickly to produce adequate mass. You only 30 minutes for the ACT. It is a speed test. Practice writing essays using a clock so that you do not run out of time.

- State your thesis in the first sentence.
- Give three supporting arguments in the first paragraph.
- Elaborate each argument, one each in the next three paragraphs.
- Conclude by reaffirming your arguments in the final paragraph.

The logical sequence criterion is met by having the three points laid out in the same order in the first paragraph, next three paragraphs, and in the conclusion.

Often, test takers get better ideas to support their thesis just when they are wrapping things up in the last paragraph. Resist the urge to add any new material or any new arguments at this point. It will violate the *logical, fully elaborated, orderly* guidelines to get a high score.

3. *The essay takes a position on the issue and may offer a critical context for discussion.*

Thesis Statement: Your essay needs a thesis statement. High scoring essays put the thesis statement up front where the grader can easily find it. Make your opening statement a simple, direct answer to the question using the wording of the question. If you are asked "Does the HPV vaccine against cervical cancer encourage promiscuous behavior," your opening sentence might be "The HPV vaccine against cervical cancer does not encourage promiscuous behavior" or state that it does promote promiscuous behavior if you want to make that argument. Make it simple, direct, and obvious so that the grader can check off the box and give you a gold star for having a clear thesis statement.

Take a position that you can develop an argument around. It does not matter which side of the issue you pick to support in your essay. Pick the side that is easier for you to turn into a verbose multi-page essay.

4. *The introduction and conclusion are effective, clear, and well developed. A clear focus on the specific issue in the prompt is maintained. Most transitions reflect the writer's logic and are usually integrated into the essay.*

Take a Position and Support It: In you first paragraph, support your thesis with three examples or three reasons. Then expand on these arguments, one in each of three following paragraphs. You need to make arguments to support your thesis, either logical arguments or use examples or anecdotal support.

On the new SAT you must assess and use information from the essay they give you to base your reply, but for the ACT, you don't need real data or facts to support your thesis, but you do need to form and support your position. You can make up reasons and data to support your contentions. They do not need to be true.

This is a writing test. It is neither a forum to state your political beliefs nor a policy recommendation that anyone cares about. Maintain focus on the prompt and on supporting your thesis. Avoid straying from the topic. If you use anecdotes, make sure they support your argument with a clear, strong point.

The Conclusion: Confidently restate (using different words) your thesis and sum up the main argument points that you have supported. As in real essays, avoid the words "in conclusion."

Although the ACT essay does not have a page limit, and you can write more, three and a half pages are sufficient. Practice planning and writing essays of sufficient bulk in the allotted time (3½ pages in 30 minutes for the ACT) so that you can be sure to have enough time to finish. A five-hundred-word essay is a reasonable goal. The ACT tends to ask practical questions rather than philosophic ones.

5. The essay shows a good command of language. Sentences are varied and word choice is varied and precise. There are few, if any, errors to distract the reader.

Vocabulary and Errors: Use vocabulary and sentence structure that you are comfortable with. Your disquisition may encourage calamity if it is comprised of extravagant vocabulary and elaborate rhetoric locution. Plain, clear English is preferable. If you don't know how to spell a word, it may be better not to use it. Take them at their word – avoid things that cause distractions. Avoid repeating the same sentence used in the first paragraph when you expand on the concept in the expository paragraphs. Try to vary the vocabulary by using adjectives and adverbs. Fully utilizing colorful adjectives can help add required bulk to your descriptions.

6. The essay addresses complexity by examining different perspectives on the issue, or by evaluating the implications and/or complications of the issue, or by fully responding to counterarguments to the writer's position.

Counterarguments: In a well-written opinion essay, you might want to provide counterarguments to show that your opinion is fair and unbiased, or just because your sun sign is Libra, and you can't help yourself.

Counterarguments, while not officially required, are usually present in ACT essays earning perfect scores. To help assure that the grader bestows points for the counterargument, make it easy to find. The most convenient spot for the counterargument is to place it as the third point in the introductory paragraph and then to support and expand on it in the third and final expository paragraph.

In the introductory paragraph, consider using wording such as, "While some might argue that" or similar words to show the grader that you have included a counterargument. In the counterargument paragraph, you should make it easy on the grader and can actually include the word "counterargument," for example, "Some who opposed voting rights for women contended that they did not have sufficient education to make informed decisions. In counterargument, many men had no formal education, yet were not prevented from voting."

Some other phrases that show a counterargument are:
- contrary to
- in spite of this
- although some may claim
- while many believe
- although some allege
- in opposition to this view

The counterargument can be a straw man. A straw man is a weak argument you set up, that is easy to tear down, and thus it appears that you have fairly considered both sides of the issue, when in fact, you have only feigned a real alternative.

Preparation

Preparation for the test essay: If you are the nervous type, you might be more comfortable writing the essay a week before the test. Read a biography on a liberal and inspirational figure, or at least study their Wikipedia page. Look up their most famous quotes and read them over a couple of times. Now, you will have some quotes and some facts to use as fillers. Then, write an essay. No matter whom you pick, there is a reasonable chance that you will be able to adapt at least a portion of the essay you have pre-written on an inspirational figure to the question on the test.

Why pick a liberal figure? The scorers are usually college students or teachers and more likely to be liberal than they are to be NRA or Tea Party members. Make them comfortable. You are free to write an essay about how Rush Limbaugh or Adolf Hitler is your hero, but if you rub the grader's noses hard enough, they may begin noticing defects they might have otherwise overlooked.

Use of details, such as dates and places, makes the essay appear more factual, even if the facts are fictitious. However, try to be plausible, especially if you use famous people or historic events. Don't cite April 5, 1947 in Barstow, California as the date and location Lincoln delivered the Gettysburg address.

It is important to do practice essays, just as much as it is important to practice other parts of the test. After practicing, evaluate your essay (or have a friend or family member score them) according to the criteria given above.

Suggested Writing Section Format

• Paragraph 1: A thesis statement, followed by an outline comprised of three arguments that support your thesis, or two supporting arguments and a counterargument.
• Paragraph 2: Expand the first argument. Maybe an example from history or literature or you may cite a research journal article, for example.
• Paragraph 3: Expand the second argument. The argument may be based on personal experience, anecdotal evidence, or from the life of a historic figure.
• Paragraph 4: Expand the third argument. This can be a counterargument and a defense.
• Paragraph 5: Conclusion. Reaffirm the thesis and make a concluding statement.

Imagination is more important than knowledge.

~Albert Einstein

CHAPTER 8: ESSAY WRITING HANDBOOK

Remember this in moments of despair. If you find that writing is hard, it's because it is hard.

~William Zinsser

It is a mistake to assume that a superior GPA and an excellent placement test score ensure admission into an elite school. These scores determine if an application merits a spot in the candidate pool or reject pile. However, having the highest GPA and ACT score in the stack will not clinch an admission either. In 2012, Harvard accepted only about one in 17 applicants. Most contenders had excellent college placement scores and high GPAs. For the most highly selective schools, applications from students with GPA's of 4.0 and ACT scores above 32 or SAT scores above 1400 are a dime-a-dozen.

Your GPA and your college placement test scores are entry criteria. If they don't meet the school's standards, it is unlikely that you'll be considered for the school. If you do make the cut, you will be among the thousands of applications from which the elite schools select a limited number of students. So how do elite schools select the most promising candidates from the pool of exceptionally bright, hard-working applicants? The essay is one critical element used to distinguish and differentiate you from the many other qualified applicants seeking the same admission spot. To surpass other applicants with similar grades and scores during winnowing, your essay needs to be a pleasure to read.

At one time, colleges used interviews to select among students applying to prestigious colleges. Admissions are much more competitive today, with many times more applicants, and using essays is more cost effective, easier to schedule, and less subject to social, racial, and other biases. Schools also use other factors to optate students; include letters of recommendation, volunteer work, extracurricular activities, publications, patents and other accomplishments. These topics are covered in other chapters.

Looking beyond your fantasies, whom would you choose to populate your ideal community? Wouldn't you pick individuals with integrity, who are responsible, thoughtful, and respect the rights of others? The great schools seek students with these attributes. Additionally, these schools are looking for insightful, creative people that will add intellectual diversity to their community, making the university a better environment for learning. They seek innovative thinkers and dreamers who are motivated and dedicated. They want students who will challenge each other and challenge the professors to examine issues with unique vision, who can find innovative solutions to problems. They are looking for leaders: social leaders and thought leaders; individuals who are willing to offer new ideas and pursue those ideas. They want students who will raise the level of the discussion. Your essay is your opportunity to display your capacity to clearly and creatively convey your ideas, and entice them with your personality.

The essay is your chance to separate yourself from other candidates who are in the top of their class in other schools. An essay that does not separate you from dozens of other bright kids is unlikely to win an acceptance letter.

For some colleges, you can doodle, compose a music score, draw, devise math equations or place anything else you choose on these pages, but most often, people write an essay. This format is most likely to work and is the format required for the Common College Application (CCA or Common App).

Whenever you compose essays for classes, think of them not as chores, but rather opportunity to hone a craft that will assist you with your college and scholarship application essays in mind. Strive to make every one of them memorable. Save them. When it comes to your application, you may have a short story or essay with a spark of passion and energy that you can rework.

Do not expect to come up with an essay that will get you placed in a selective school with 48 hours to go before your application deadline. There is a book available on how to write your college essay in an hour. If your have test scores and GPA well above the level that the college you are applying for expects, almost any essay will do. One written in the waning hours before the deadline will complete the requirements of your application. In this case, it's best just to complete an essay and get it submitted. However, if you hope to get into a selective school or if your choice school is a stretch, you will want to do better.

It does not take copious hours or a gargantuan effort to create a great essay. However, it does take time. Good writing is like good wine. The grapes are crushed, the must allowed to ferment, and the juice separated. Still it is not ready; the wine needs to settle, be filtered, age, and be bottled. Hasty winemaking begets an insipid or acrid brew. Lacking care, it may turn to vinegar. Good writing requires the passage of time, allowing the essay to rest, refine, and mature.

AEFS (Admission Essay Fatigue Syndrome) is a disease endemic among college admission officers. Their job includes two months during which they read thousands of sophomoric essays. The unfortunate essay readers are victim to hundreds of boring essays. Be considerate to these brave souls; no one wants to choke down another essay about grandma, unless it is an exposé of her days running a brothel, or her clandestine adventures undermining the communist regime of Soviet Russia.

Admission officers assess your intellect from your placement scores and GPA. Your letters of recommendation should assure them that you play well with others. The essays (including the extracurricular activity essay) can create a sense of person, revealing aspects not seen in other areas of the application.

- Avoid content that reiterates material found elsewhere in your application.
- Avoid sob stories, your love life, your winning touchdown, flaunting of your public consciousness, and things in your remote past (unless relevant to recent transformations).
- Don't use the essay to explain away your imperfections and poor grades, make excuses, complain about evil teachers (other than to praise them), or whine about how rough life has been. Don't be a loser.
- Don't make a list of your accomplishments or brag about your achievements. Do not talk about yourself in third-person; likewise, limit the number of times you use the word "I."
- Humor is welcome, but unless you are applying to clown college, avoid puns, off-color humor, and jokes.

An author paints characters through their reactions to events. It is not the event that makes a character interesting; different people react differently to the same occurrence. You do not need a tremendous event to portray tremendous character. Common events can do this. What choices have you made; did you make the obvious one? Reaction to failure may be more revealing than reaction to triumph.

The essay should tell a story that conveys who you are, one which reveals a sense of wonder and appreciation, that shows what you care about, and how you approach life. The essay may be a story that manifests your judgment and values, or reveals the choices you have made. Don't make the focus what you have done or what has happened to you.

All great adventure stories include danger, conflict, and a decision point at which the hero chooses personal hazard for the greater good. In most stories, the hero starts out as a lowly apprentice who is baffled at being selected for a position they feel they do not merit or even want. In the archetypal hero story, the protagonist overcomes their personal weaknesses and destroys the nefarious villain, exceeding the skill of their mentor, who had been unable to defeat the malfeasant fiend.

If you are going to be a hero, you need to include flaws and self-doubt, and the moment of transition where you overcame your weakness. There is nothing exciting about Superman staying home and lifting 1000-pound weights. It is evocative when he has self-doubts and conflicts, makes hard choices, and decides to take on personal risks to defend those he loves and the ideals in which he believes. If he has no flaws or weaknesses, there is no story.

Without kryptonite, you got nothing.

Jon Stewart

Don't use the essay to highlight achievements that you have included elsewhere in your application or to brag about your accomplishments. Allow others do that for you in letters of recommendation, or cite your accomplishments in your résumé.

The essay however is a place to acknowledge growth. Write a story about overcoming conflict or adversity and tough choices you have made. Allow yourself to betray your secret doubts, to briefly expose flaws or failings for a singular lucid moment, which you then re-shroud within a knight's armor. Divulging an epiphany, a transcendent experience that shattered the warped mirror of ego, demonstrates that you welcome transformation. Revealing a vulnerable moment, that imbued your life with tragedy and redemption, shows depth of character.

If writing about someone who influenced your life, don't lavish adulation like an infatuated adolescent; portray a real person, an unlikely hero that overcame flaws to achieve what you respect in them. Alternatively, relate how you were influenced by an antihero, disillusioned by a fallen hero, or followed a person, whose behavior you later rejected, whose path you renounced to save yourself. But, did you try to change them? Did you abandon them without saying why? Was that cowardice on your part?

When you have the option, write stories for your English classes about times when you have gone against the flow of what was expected to help someone, even though you were frightened; or had an adventure because you took a risk, even one you later regretted. Write about a situation where you were unexpectedly forced out of your comfort zone; and the consequences of that. If you have never challenged yourself or challenged authority, or if you have never taken a risk to help someone, maybe it's time to do so. Saving kittens is far too cliché unless you reflect how foolish it was to risk your life for it. Look for humor in your darkest moments; that humor may be irony. Alternatively, perhaps relate how a series of innocuous, insignificant decisions converged to change your life.

- Write three essays – then pick the best to perfect.
- Ask yourself if 1000 others have written a similar essay.
- Make sure that your essay has a theme and makes a point.

Write in first person. In expository essays, you want your opinions to be objective, or at least to appear objective. You may have been instructed to avoid writing in first person, to help convey a more authoritative, impartial voice. The admission essay, however, is usually about you. Who knows you better? This is supposed to be an honest reflection of you as a person. Writing in the first person, you are more likely to come across as yourself.

Avoid generalities. Specifics make you sound knowledgeable and make a story feel more real and intense. "It wasn't any morning; it was June 16th, the morning of my mother's surgery." Already, the reader knows that there is unpleasant anticipation. Personalize your story. If it includes the names of your favorite haunts and friends, it helps creates a sense of authenticity.

Make the reading painless; avoiding tedious or redundant prose. Do not hammer the reader with platitudes. The purpose is not to impress with the largest of your intellect, but rather to illustrate your ability to communicate clearly. Tell your story in a way that is fun to read. Humor, even dark humor, is much better than dreary or drab.

Beginning an essay or story in the midst of action creates a sense of excitement. Often, the opening sentences can be lopped off, thus beginning the story in the middle, shortening the piece, and giving it velocity. Try to hook the reader in the first moments. Get to the point quickly so that the reader is oriented and has context for understanding where they are headed. Otherwise, the writing can seem like aimless word soup.

Show; don't tell. Don't make a report of what is happening; create a scene for the reader. We are not whom we say we are; we are what we do. Paint a picture with action or inaction.

His eyes fixed and glazed, illuminated by the blue flicker of reruns; he slouched in a ratty recliner, filling his mouth with stale chips and slurping tepid flat cola, savoring none of it.

A limited amount of dialog can set the stage for the topic and create a hook. Nevertheless, keep dialog limited. "She told you in a text?!!" would be sufficient dialog to set the stage for a story.

Keep the essay to the word or page limit, and follow directions; your ability to follow directions is part of the test. The Common App (CCA) essay must be 250 to 650 words or you will get an error message when you try to save it. Review it, and have at least two other people review it, to eliminate any spelling, grammar, or other errors. You only get so many words; choose them wisely.

Please, do not write an ACT placement test style 1:3:1, five paragraph expository essay as described in Chapter 7 for your college admission essay. The same goes for scholarship essays.

The secret to great writing is rewriting and rewriting again. Revise and rewrite until you can't stand to do it again, then wait at least a few days and then, rewrite again. Author and teacher of writing, William Zinsser, concludes that there is no such thing as good writing, only good rewriting. Your prose should be clear and understandable. It should be easy to read and comprehend. It should be fun, not drudgery. Perhaps, you do not savor the style in which this book is written. If not, consider how poorly written and what a painful read it was eleven revisions ago.

Rewriting goes beyond simply eliminating errors and redundancy. Avoid clichés and dull, overused, hackneyed phrases. The language should be fresh and varied. Rearrange paragraphs and eliminate deadwood to improve flow. Eliminate pointless divergences and build bridges where needed to keep your reader from getting lost. Each sentence should be a pleasure. Ensure that the story path leads out of the woods and into the light.

Use vocabulary you are familiar with and that is natural to you. Don't be pretentious. Trying to impress readers with super-syllabic jargon is likely to annoy rather than entertain, especially if the words are ill-suited to your intention. Use words that most precisely convey the sentiment or meaning you intend. Avoid using unnatural language, as it will likely sound ...unnatural. Unusual word choices slow comprehension and slow the flow of your writing.

Don't nictitate when you can wink, nor imbibe if you can drink. Don't attenuate if you can shrink, nor ratiocinate if you can think.

Have fun with language. A thesaurus can help you create color and music in your writing. When dabbling with color, don't settle for the eight color crayon box; buttercup, marigold, and daffodil paint a different image than sulfur, mustard, or neon yellow. Try to vary your vocabulary to increase interest. Alliteration can give lilt, flow, and humor with sound. Don't use a thesaurus to find big words; use it to find great ones.

Eschew arcane, impenetrable cants. Eloquence is not the creation of complex rhetoric, but rather the ability to elucidate and expose complex concepts with elegant clarity.

Making the simple complicated is commonplace; making the complicated simple, awesomely simple, that's creativity.
~Charles Mingus

Read your work aloud to see if it flows easily. If you cannot read it without stumbling, it's likely the result of clumsy construction. Avoid ceding to sentences you would never say.

Be ~~ever so~~ frugal with your words; ~~and~~ eliminate those ~~that are~~ unneeded. Add detail. Eliminate clutter.

Avoid compound sentences when they are not needed. A sentence should have one idea. Try to limit compound sentences to those that need to be married to convey causation and linkage. Otherwise, don't use one sentence where two will do.

Microsoft Word or other word processors have spell- and grammar-checking tools. These are great for showing basic errors. However, use caution when eliminating those red and green jagged lines; not everything marked is wrong, not everything that goes unmarked is correct. Use the underlined markings to review your writing, but be cautious: it would be an error to blindly banish split infinitives or all passive voice from your prose. Not every word will be in the spell check dictionary.

The use of expletive construction *is a* stylistic error *that is* wordy and *that is* boring. This commonly occurs with overuse of pronouns and forms of the verb "to be" (is, are, was, were....). Review your essay and eliminate these when possible. (*Expletive construction results in wordy, boring writing.*) Avoid overuse of the verb "to be"; consider whether stronger, more descriptive verbs might improve your writing.

Use caution with pronouns and the passive voice when more than one character acts in a paragraph or scene. Pronouns and the passive voice can introduce confusion in understanding who is the subject or object of the action. Make sure that the noun represented by the pronoun is obvious.

Avoid excessive adverbs. Adverbs can make writing wordy and weak. Example: *Tightly* holding her child's hand, she *hurriedly* moved out the door, calling *loudly* for help. Rewritten: Grasping her child's hand, she rushed out the door and cried for help.

If you find that you are using numerous "*ly*" words or other adverbs, replace them with verbs that are more descriptive. Refrain from using unneeded, redundant adverbs such as "tightly clutching" or "screaming loudly." When was the last time you clutched something loosely?

Basically, in *most* circumstances, it is *often* better, to avoid *when possible*, as many hedge words as you *reasonably* can. *In general,* hedge words *may actually* weaken the writer's message.

Hedge words are used to weaken statements; often to deceive. They may weaken statements even when used as intensifiers: I *really* love my job, adds an unnecessary and weakening qualifier. Always avoid double hedges. In the following contrivance, a manager fires an employee to clean up an embarrassing failure.

Someone is likely responsible for doing something, at some point, which may have allowed thieves to enter the building, perhaps explaining the disappearance of the data. Admittedly, it may appear someone might have possibly implied you were somehow partially responsible. Nevertheless, it is utterly and categorically denied that your dismissal represents even an iota of accusation of possible culpability on your part.

Hedge words, however, can increase persuasiveness, especially in technical writing, when required to describe facts accurately.

Finally, read your essay as if someone was paying you $20 for every error you can find. Read it aloud. Watch out for changes in tense, look for subject-verb disagreements; check your punctuation, grammar, and spelling. Expect to rewrite it at least five times, hopefully, having time to let the essay rest a week before a final revision.

Reading Level Score Tip: Most word processors calculate reading complexity scores. Microsoft Word gives Readability Statistics after completing the Spelling and Grammar check. It provides scores for percent passive sentences, the Flesch Reading *Ease* score, and the Flesch-Kincaid *Grade* level score.

Ease and Grade scores are based on the number of syllables per word and the number of words per sentence. The Reading-Ease test gives more weight to the number of syllables. These tests tell nothing about how well written an essay is. Nevertheless, they cast light on readability. For literature, it is best to keep the number of passive sentences low to maintain clarity. An ease score of 70 percent and a 7th-grade reading level provide pleasant, fluid, adult level reading.

In scoring successful Harvard admission essays, I found that passive sentence counts were, with rare exception, 9% or less. Most essays had reading Ease scores over 55 percent. Almost all were above the 7th-grade reading level. The most enjoyable essays had Ease scores of 70% and scored at the 8th-grade reading level. A few successful Harvard admission essays had as many as 25% passive sentences. One had a 35.5% ease level and a grade level of 17.1. However, these were not great reads. These essays made me wonder if the students gained acceptance in spite of their essays.

Excellent admission essays usually have an ease and grade score product of at least five. (Example: 70.5% times 8.1 = 5.71). This seems to be a sweet spot for clarity and readability. In these essays, the sentences and vocabulary were pleasant and varied and carried the reader's interest.

Scholarship Essays: When applying for scholarships, be even more careful to follow directions and avoid errors. Hundreds of applications may be submitted for just a few scholarships. Broken rules, late applications, and slipshod work are all reasons to eliminate your application. You can lighten the reviewer's workload by not following directions, and thus allow them to eliminate your application, simplifying their task of winnowing the many candidates. Read the rules and follow them. Get your application in before the deadline. Use the format they request.

If submitting paper applications or résumés, make sure they are neat, clean, and well organized with headings and page numbers if applicable. If it looks like it was a last minute effort, has typos, is crumpled or stained, the reviewer may assume your application was not a high priority in your life. Go the extra mile to make your paperwork appear professional.

Application Essay Prompts

The CCA essay simplifies the task of essay writing as one essay is used for applications to multiple schools. For schools that do not utilize the CCA, it may be tempting to adapt your essay for other applications. Be careful to make sure your essay addresses the question in the prompt. The CCA prompts change from year to year. Take a look at them early on, to decide what you want to write about. Some colleges using the CCA require additional essays. If you apply to the University of Chicago, you will have an unusual essay challenge.

To be yourself in a world that is constantly trying to make you something else is the greatest accomplishment.

~Ralph Waldo Emerson

A masterpiece can be painted on any canvas.

~Charly Lewis

CHAPTER 9: COMMUNITY SERVICE

No one cares how much you know, until they know how much you care.

~Theodore Roosevelt

Many schools and scholarships look for students that have demonstrated concern for something beyond their personal, narrow self-interest; they look favorably upon students that have volunteered to perform community service.

If your community service is limited to picking up litter along the roadside, it may be confused with the community service hours a judge mandates following a first offence. You could log those hours; however, the service you report on your application should be service that reveals your interests and commitment. While hours are counted, it is not the hours, but rather the dedication those hours demonstrate that is important.

Community service can and should be an activity where you utilize your creativity, initiative, and leadership. It is best when the service is an excuse to have fun.

Fun and community service in the same sentence? Yes! This should be your goal. Think about things that you enjoy doing, things you care about. Your volunteer work should either be so much fun that you are glad to do it or should give you such a warm glow inside that you would do it again.

It may be work, even hard work. However, it should be a positive experience for you. It should not be something that you do just to fill some hours on a form or fulfill a requirement. Don't expect a staged photo-op, pretending to be washing dishes at a soup kitchen, to impress anyone.

When you put your service down on paper, your joy, and sense of accomplishment should shine through. If the experience was an unpleasant chore that you were reluctant to do, it will likely show through to the scholarship or admission committee. They want to give money and accept people into their programs whom they believe will continue to contribute to society. They are looking for people who want to do something with their lives. If you do things because you have to, things you never want to repeat, they may recognize this reading between the lines of your description. Just seeking out activities you enjoy, shows that you are ready to take direction in your life.

- Do you love canoeing? Volunteer to teach canoeing to kids at a summer camp.
- Do you rejoice in playing music? Volunteer to play music at charity events, or teach music to kids in summer programs.
- Like to build things? Try Habitat for Humanity if you are over 16.
- Exalt in the sunshine? Volunteer as a camp counselor for a non-profit summer camp on the Florida coast, or volunteer to build trails in a park.
- Relish cooking? Volunteer in the kitchen at a homeless shelter or do a barbeque for fund raising event.
- Do you have a flair for theater? Volunteer to work with kids at a summer or after-school program doing a play. Do make-up for a charity pageant. Read aloud to children in a library program or to the elderly in a nursing home.
- Prefer computers to people? Almost every charity needs IT and computer maintenance help; however, you might consider an activity that grows your people skills.
- Love animals? Volunteer at an animal shelter or a wildlife rehabilitation center.

Volunteering does not have to be limited to fun stuff; it is also about things worth doing. Helping people get their lives back in order after a storm by helping clean up their homes is a great gift.

It can be dirty, sweaty work, but can give a great sense of accomplishment.

My niece did a coat drive for homeless and needy families. She visited several local fast food joints, explained her plan, and they gave her coupons. For the restaurants, it was a bargain – they donated coupons for free servings of fries or beverages. In return, they were able to sell meals to hungry teenagers. My niece then got a coat drive announced on the high school morning bulletin. For donating a clean, used, unneeded winter coat that was crowding their closets at home, students would receive a coupon for free, fast food. She collected 350 winter coats, donated in a single day, for needy families. She helped keep hundreds of people warm for the winter with a few hours of free time.

While you are in high school, you are likely to have the freedom to volunteer for the kind of job that you would love. Most high school students do not have to worry about paying rent or buying groceries. However, that day comes soon for almost all of us. If you can work without pay, it is easier to find a position as an apprentice in a field for which experience is hard to garner. This kind of experience opens new opportunities. Although it may not be community service, if you can volunteer to do this type of work for a non-profit organization, it may be counted as such.

Having volunteer experience working with injured animals gives evidence that you have a realistic idea of what being a veterinarian would be like. This will be valuable if you hope to apply to veterinary school in the future. On the other hand, you may find that you are completely ill-suited to the profession you had aspired to, and decide to take a different path. I have friends that graduated medical school and spent years in residency training, only to realize that they were ill-adapted or unhappy practicing medicine.

If you are volunteering with the goal of accumulating community service hours for school or a scholarship program, make sure that your school will recognize the hours, and that the organization will give you a letter stating the number of hours of service you provided. Verify that the hours will qualify for community service beforehand, to ensure that you will not be disappointed later when it may be too late to perform the required hours.

If you have a passion, find a way to turn it not only into community service hours you enjoy, but also into an opportunity to develop skills that will serve you and help you serve the people around you. *People skills are among the most important skills required for success in life.* Volunteering, with a sincere interest in helping those you work with, is a great way to grow your people skills and self-confidence.

After you complete your community service hours and write about your experience, you can prevaricate, telling how you gained much more from the experience and from the people you helped than what you gave to them. The humble attitude goes over great.

On the other hand, it could be the truth.

As a Peace Corps volunteer, I spent two arduous years engaged in community development service in an isolated, impoverished, insular area. The village was a dozen miles from the nearest paved road, and without the benefit of running water, plumbing, electricity, or telephone. The only electronic devices were battery-powered radios retorting indigenous music. The ignorance, even to basic hygiene, was bewildering. In the village of over 1000 people, there was one toilet and about three or four outhouses. Most people defecated in the bushes. When a child became ill, it was assumed the result witchcraft. Each task of daily living was a challenge. Effecting change within the community was a multiple of that. It was a dangerous environment, with treacherous roads, finicky military and corrupt police. There were several incidents, and a couple of diseases, I feel fortunate, in retrospect, to have survived.

Living and working with the people of my host country was a tremendous pleasure, and those years provided me an incredible, transformational experience. They remain two of the most valued years of my life. The self-confidence I developed, the understanding of myself, and the experience of immersion in a different culture opened my horizons to set goals and to accomplish things I would have not considered possible for me, having previously assumed them out of reach.

It's funny to see Peace Corps volunteers portrayed in popular media. They are often shown in bikinis on a beach or on a yacht, drinking cocktails in a lush tropical vacation spot. This may reflect a couple of vacation days out of two years of service. The rest of the time, it is "the toughest job you'll ever love."

What lies behind us and what lies before us are tiny matters compared to what lies within us.

~Ralph Waldo Emerson

But of course, we can't take any credit for our talents. It's how we use them that counts.

~Mrs. Whatsit
A Wrinkle in Time

There is nothing courageous in being fearless. Courage is not being fearless, but rather facing challenges in spite of your fear.

~Dorothy Gale
of Oz

CHAPTER 10: ACADEMIC SCHOLARSHIPS

You are the only person on earth who can use your ability.

~Zig Ziglar

It does not take a super grade point average or extraordinary scholastic or athlete skill to win scholarships. Although these attributes don't hurt, many scholarships don't ask about grades or limit themselves to students with a high GPA. Some require nothing more than an essay. To join Mensa International, you must prove you have a genius IQ. To win their scholarship just takes an essay. Other scholarships don't even require that.

There are, however, elements that determine which students receive scholarships: maturity and organization. Most students do not receive scholarships for the simple reason that they do not apply for them. They wait too long. They lack self-confidence. They lack initiative. They are not used to filling out forms. Most students, even great students, are not proactive, only reactive to teacher's deadlines. They may be able to get their school assignments in on time, but applying for scholarships takes initiative. The key to getting scholarships is applying.

A young woman I know received more scholarships than the rest of her graduating class combined. She was not the top student in her class and never struck me as particularly articulate or urbane. She was, however, a dedicated and diligent student, and most importantly, she applied for numerous scholarships. She passionately described her goals and convinced the scholarship committees their goals would be well served by her. She likely won less than one in five of those she applied for.

Most college-bound students can, with dedication, win more college financing per hour, investing time into applying for scholarships than they can by working in a minimum wage job. There is no guarantee, but it can have a much better payout.

There are nearly as many scholarships available as there are high school students starting university each year. Some are limited to college major, town of residence, ethnicity, even to last name. Most of these are not full scholarships, and most are small: less than $2000. You can increase your chances, as this girl did, by applying for several. It is OK to win more than one.

Scholarships are often limited to college major, town of residence, ethnicity, even to last name. Don't waste time applying for computer engineering scholarships if you plan to major in art or biology.

An outstanding application is much more likely to win than one thrown together that merely completes the required components. High grades and ACT/SAT scores never hurt, but don't assume you are not eligible if you are not a top student.

While many scholarships are extremely competitive, some scholarships go un-awarded because no one has applied. This is particularly true of local scholarships or others restricted to very specific criteria. They may be limited to a population group that includes you. There are many programs, in which the number of scholarships awarded is close to the number of applicants.

As a student, you should realize that the application is a test. The kids that get the scholarships, and that get into the great schools, do so by applying in time, and by submitting a quality application. It works out. The kids who are mature enough to get into the great schools, and who will utilize those scholarships effectively are those who are mature and resourceful enough to get a quality application in on time.

NOTE TO PARENTS: Your child may need assistance in organizing time and effort for applying for college and scholarships. It requires a level of maturity many 12th graders have not yet attained.

Although there are a few scholarships available to high school freshmen and sophomores, and several available for juniors, the majority are available to high school seniors, with more available and many more available students already enrolled in college. Begin your search by your junior year.

- Apply for scholarships you are eligible for.
- Follow the rules.
- Get the application in by the deadline.

If applying by mail, make sure your application packet is neat and attractive, that you follow formatting rules, and that your application is orderly and presentable. This means no soup stains on the essay. Your name should be in the header or footer of each page, and pages should be numbered.

Several internet scholarship search sites are available for helping you find scholarships. For most of these, you must register and give information so that they can match you to the appropriate scholarships. The sites need information to narrow down the massive number of scholarships in their database to those you would be eligible for. They request information such as whether you are Hispanic or the child of a police officer; they ask your GPA, where you live, your gender, extracurricular activities, religion and numerous other factors that determine your eligibility for specific scholarships. There are scholarships limited by religious affiliation, by parent's profession, or even by last name. There are scholarships for students that participate in a wide range of activates including archery, dance, song writing, cartoon drawing, and beach volleyball. The search site cannot match you to a rodeo scholarship if they don't know that you are rodeo-active. Nonetheless, if there is information requested you do not want to reveal about yourself and family, feel free to leave those parts blank.

Several scholarship sites are legitimate businesses providing a great free service. As such, they have to make money, and some of the sites do so by showing you or sending you advertisements. Others sell your information. Some will fill your email box and your home mailbox with mail and offers. Other scholarship sites are scams intent on defrauding you.

If you want to carefully put your toe in the water and check out a site, you can give temporary registration data, and even use a temporary email address. These sites may ask for some sensitive data, such as family income. When registering using your real name and data, be sure to look for the check box that may give them permission to send advertisements to your email or home mailbox. I suggest that you uncheck at least the email box so that you are not inundated by junk mail, unless it is an email that you created specifically for this purpose. In this case, don't plan to use it for anything else.

I maintain a separate email account just for registering at sites that I suspect will get me spammed. Gmail and Yahoo are very good at eliminating most mass volume spam, but will not prevent junk mail sent to you as an individual.

The most well know and most favored scholarship sites include:

Fastweb.com
CollegeBoard.com
CollegeNet.com
Scholarships.com
SallieMae
SchoolSoup.com
ScholarshipMonkey.com

SchoolSoup and ScholarshipMonkey will use the addresses you supply to send you email and snail mail from third parties and may sell your information unless you are careful to opt out while signing up. Look for the small box about receiving third party offers, and make sure you don't give them rights to use your information, unless that is what you want.

To get the widest listing of scholarships you may be eligible for, use at least two of these services to search for opportunities. Different sites are likely to find at least a few different prospects for you.

Smaller scholarships:

Help with paying for college is great, and winning scholarships breeds success. If you get even a small scholarship (even if it is only $500), it certifies you a winner. We all love to be on the winning team and schools and scholarship boards are no different. When they see you have won other awards, it provides evidence that you are a winner and a doer and that you may be a good investment of their funds. Winning even a small scholarship gives you an award to put on your C.V. and college applications. If may increase your odds of winning future scholarships, getting into a more selective college and graduate school, and may even help you get a better job upon graduation. Thus, it can be worth the effort to apply for even small awards, especially if you have not won any others yet.

Beware of Scholarship Scams

There are many scholarship scammers to avoid. These thieves prey on unsuspecting students. They may steal money by charging fees, through identity theft, by selling your information, or through other forms of fraud. Here are some things that should alert you to a scam to be avoided:

- If they charge any fees.
- If they say you must act immediately, when there is not published deadline.
- If they guarantee you will win a scholarship.
- If they request personal financial or account data.
- If they ask for a bank account number, credit card information, or social security number.

- If they are a fake federal agency. (The only federal college scholarships are for military academies and the ROTC.)
- If they call you on the phone, especially if you didn't apply.
- If you do a web search and don't find a website that has a telephone number to contact them.
- If they say that they will apply for you.
- If it sounds too good to be true.

If you suspect something is a scam, do a Google search of the name or description of the organization along with the word "scam". If it is a scam, odds are you are not the first person to be approached, and you will find out about them with a web search.

I recently received a phone call telling me my computer had a virus, and that they would help me get rid of it. I immediately thought "Cool, a scam I had not heard of before." Instead of going to the website, they directed me to; I did a Google search for the site along with the word "scam." Google immediately came up with a description of the fraudulent scheme being attempted. If I had followed their instructions, I would have given them access to all the passwords on my computer, along with security data, personal data, bank account and credit card numbers.

Be wary of scams and check out anything and anyone that offers you something you did not earn. Remember that scammers prosper by appealing to greed and sloth.

Other Scholarships

Your church, organizations you belong to, your parents' employers, local businesses, and local organizations may have scholarships funds you are eligible for. These scholarships often have few other applicants. Local scholarships sometimes do not receive a single application. Ask around. Your high school counselor may be aware of local scholarships available only to students in your town. The college you plan to attend likely has scholarships available only to students who attend that school.

Don't assume scholarships are only for high school seniors. There are numerous scholarships available only to students who are already enrolled in college. There are also scholarships reserved for graduate students working on master, doctoral, and postdoctoral programs.

Not all scholarships are for college. There are scholarships for summer internships, training programs, oversees experiences and leadership programs. Don't overlook these opportunities.

Beware of certain commercial for-profit college scholarships. The purpose of these is to lure students into commercial schools. Often, these scholarships dry up or require maintenance of an unrealistic GPA. In some of these programs, most students have lost their scholarship by the end of the first semester, and end up paying full tuition. If a scholarship requires a GPA of 3.5 or above, it should be suspect, especially at a private, for-profit school.

Some scholarships require documentation showing admission into college. Thus, to be eligible for those scholarships, you need to have already secured admission into at least one school. If the scholarship is for a targeted field of study, it may require admission into the department of that discipline. For example, to eligible for some engineering scholarships, the candidate needs to have already been admitted into an engineering program. Thus, it is strategic to apply for early action (not necessarily restrictive early decision) into a college program where you are confident you can gain admission. This will make you eligible for a wider set of scholarships, even if that school is not your first choice for your university education.

Energy and persistence conquer all things.

~Benjamin Franklin

CHAPTER 11: SPORTS SCHOLARSHIPS

You must have long-range goals to keep you from being frustrated by short-range failures.

~Charles C. Noble

Over a million young men play high school football; less than one in 50 gets a football scholarship. Over six hundred thousand young women participate in high school track and field, but there are only about 4,500 college athletic scholarships for these sports.

A sports scholarship is not free money. With most academic scholarships, as long as you maintain a reasonable GPA, you will receive the scholarship funds you won. With a sports scholarship, you have to continue spending time practicing and playing the sport.

The scholarship is a bonus if your goal is to play college sports and something you would pay to do. However, if your performance is not good enough, or if you are injured and can't perform, the scholarship will be given to someone else. I had a friend who was attending a private college on a dance scholarship. She broke her ankle, and the scholarship evaporated.

Playing competitive sports at the college level requires many hours of practice each week, year round, as well as travel for games. The sport will compete with time you would be studying or doing other activities. It is not a bargain. If you don't love it, a sports scholarship is a low-paying job without disability insurance. Even if you do play college ball, unless you are exceptionally talented and can avoid injury, your chances of playing professional sports is low. About one percent of college basketball players and about two percent of college football players make it onto professional teams. The best bet is baseball, where nearly 12% of male college players play professional baseball; however, the majority of these are minor league players. Sadly, the risk of lifelong injury from playing high school and college sports is vastly greater than the chances of going pro.

Contrary to what you may expect, few sports scholarships are full rides. Other than basketball and football, the average sports scholarship is less than $9,000 per year, and many provide only a couple thousand dollars. Mostly, they help pay part of the Expected Family Contribution (see Chapter 18), so most college athletes actually rely more on financial aid than their sports scholarship. Depending on the college the student attends, it might be cheaper to go to an in-state college, and forgo the sports scholarship. Lower income students might pay the same for an in-state education without the scholarship.

What the athletic scholarship can do, is help the student get into a college that they might not have been accepted to if they did not have their athletic abilities. Athletic prowess and playing college sports may make up for some weakness in their GPA or placement test scores. These abilities, however, rarely help the student pass tests or graduate. Class work and preparing for the ACT are more effective use of time for those who hope to attend and graduate from a great college.

Sports scholarships are neither charity nor altruistic means of increasing student body diversity. They are part of the university's business plan. A winning sports team attracts non-athlete students to the school, making it seem a fun place to attend. You should be aware that if you play competitive college sports, you are being exploited as part of the school's recruitment efforts. The scholarships are just an entertainment advertisement cost for the school.

Division III schools are not allowed to offer sports scholarships, but they do have competitive sports teams. These are typically smaller colleges. Playing sports at these schools usually requires a less-demanding training schedule, which may be limited to practice during the sports playing season. These schools often offer academic and leadership scholarships or other need- or merit-based financial aid to students, including athletes. Although there are no athletic scholarships, they like to recruit athletes. This can provide an athlete the opportunity to participate in competitive sports, but usually with less pressure than in Division I or II schools. As an added benefit, you can't lose an athletic scholarship you didn't win. If you want to play college sports because you love the game, Division III schools may be the sweet spot to do it.

As a physician, I strongly encourage physical activity and athleticism. Team sports can be fun, and athletics is a place for personal challenge and development. However, rather than competitive or team sports, I encourage students to participate in lifetime sports which can be continued throughout life for fitness and enjoyment. These include swimming, tennis, cross country running, golf, and dance. Once you're out of school, there is little opportunity to be a linebacker or tight end. Consider opportunities you have now to learn sports that you can practice on you own or with a friend, sports that you will be able to do for years.

If you love a sport and want to play it, that's great; follow your dream. However, be realistic about sports as a means of paying for college and the odds that it will provide a career for you. Few students become professional athletes, and most of those only play a couple of seasons. Athletic scholarships should not be considered a free ride through college, but rather a tough, demanding, and dangerous, low-paying job with limited long-term career opportunities.

Nothing great was ever achieved without enthusiasm.

~Ralph Waldo Emerson

CHAPTER 12: U.S. MILITARY SERVICE-FINANCED EDUCATIONAL

If your actions inspire others to dream more, learn more, do more and become more, you are a leader.

~John Quincy Adams

There are four paths to having your college education paid for in part or entirely by the military. Not all these are equal.

- You go through a U.S. military academy, graduate, and become an officer.
- You enroll in the ROTC program at a college campus in the United States, graduate, and become an officer.
- You join the Army Reserve and some college costs are paid while you are in the Reserve.
- You join the military and get educational GI benefits later.

Military Academies

The U.S military academies are among the most exclusive and highest rated colleges in the world, don't cost a penny, and provide full tuition, housing, and meals. They are not free, however, as they include a commitment and commission into the military as an officer. If this is something you want to do, it is a tremendous opportunity. When you graduate, you will have a job in the field of your training, responsibility, and gain practical and leadership experience that transfers into civilian life.

It is not easy to gain entry into a military academy. It requires superior grades and a recommendation from a member of congress. These academies are not for the faint of heart, weak of mind or frail constitution: enrollment includes a rigorous boot camp prior to admittance into the programs.

There are four undergraduate academies: Annapolis for the Navy, West Point for the U.S. Army, the Air Force Academy, and the Coast Guard Academy. There are also several other military colleges and junior colleges. There is a military medical and nursing school. If you would like to run cruise ships or oil tankers, there are several merchant marine academies in the U.S. as well. These are considerably less competitive.

ROTC Programs

Each branch of the military has a college ROTC (reserve officer training corps) program. In these programs, students study in regular colleges. Although exemplary personal behavior is expected of the ROTC students, campus life is less restrictive than it is in a military academy. Along with other classes, ROTC members receive special leadership training courses. Most colleges grant credit hours for these courses.

The ROTC program provides scholarships, which often give a full ride through college with a guaranteed military job in the field of your training upon graduation. As with the academies, graduates become military officers; have responsibility, and gain practical and leadership experience that have great value in civilian life.

Most ROTC scholarships pay full tuition costs, a living allowance of $300 to $500 a month, and a book allowance. Additionally, many colleges give additional ROTC benefits, such as free on-campus housing. ROTC scholarships continue to be available after starting college.

The military is looking for individuals with integrity and leadership experience, so demonstrated leadership and good citizenship during high school will help in gaining an ROTC scholarship. The academic requirements for ROTC are not out of reach for most students and are nowhere as high as they are for the military academies.

Each branch of the military has its own ROTC program, each has slightly different academic requirements, and each is interested in students pursuing different career fields. For example, the Army ROTC only requires a GPA of 2.75 and an ACT of 19, while the Air Force requires a GPA of 3.0 and an ACT score of 24 to be eligible for the scholarships.

The ROTC programs are available at seven senior military colleges (SMC) as well as at hundreds of regular college campuses. The acceptance criteria (GPA and placement scores) depend on the school. The degrees are mostly technical, such as nursing and various branches of engineering, but also include management, public affairs, law, foreign languages, atmospheric science, petroleum engineering, oceanography, divinity, band directing, aircraft piloting, and many others. The degrees the military branches look for depend upon their mission needs. All students at the SMC may take ROTC training but may opt out of military service if they do not take ROTC scholarships. SMC schools include Texas A&M, Virginia Tech, and the Citadel.

Military academies and the ROTC consider varsity sports a plus on an applicant's CV. These sports evince the applicant's physical prowess, competitiveness, ability to work as a team, and even leadership. These are traits prized by the military.

The Army Reserve

A third route to have military service help pay for a college education is the Army Reserve. There are various programs, including some that will pay-off up to $50,000 in college loans for a 6-year enlistment. If you enlist before or during college, the Army Reserve will pay up to $250 per credit hour, up to $4500 per academic year. This is much less than the tuition cost for most colleges. There are also "pay" benefits for soldiers for up to 36 months of education, which can amount to $12,420 and up to an additional $25,020 under certain circumstances. It would be hard to survive through college on this amount.

Enlisted into the Army Reserves and National Guard can suddenly become active foot soldiers or sailors in the Navy. They start boot camp at the lowest rank, and if there is a war or conflict, get to go as a soldier. Reserve members have seen more tours-of-duty than regular Army soldiers have in recent years. Educational benefits during the active duty period are of little benefit, as it may be impossible to attend class or take tests while deployed to Afghanistan or other remote location. Additionally, benefits can be lost if grades are not maintained or if the enlistee gains weight. The Army may rescind payment to the college mid-semester, and if the student can't come up with the cash to pay the tuition themselves– they can lose the semester's work.

Enlist First – Study Later

A fourth way military service will pay for college education is to join the military. When your contract is over, the military may pay some of your college costs. What they pay changes over time, depending on government funding. Currently, these benefits amount to a fraction of the cost of attending a four-year college.

The military will also give you training. Most soldiers have support functions rather than being trained primarily to engage in combat as seen in movies. Support functions include medics, truck drivers, cooks, and equipment repair, along with numerous other jobs. Unfortunately, military training usually does not transfer directly to civilian certification. Even though a soldier may have done the job for two years under harsh and dangerous war zone conditions, they often need to complete a certification course from the beginning to do similar work in civilian clothing.

CAUTION: Oftentimes, military recruiter's promises about field of training and benefits are not kept. Other shenanigans are sometimes used to deny benefits. A young woman I know was released from active duty with one day less than two-year requirement for educational benefits completed; she would have received no benefits if she had not reenlisted for four more years!

If you are joining the military to get help paying for college, make sure you get the agreement in writing. If the recruiter promises training in a specific area that is of interest to you, get it in writing. Talk to people who have been through the process to learn the pitfalls and traps. Some people love their military experience; others hate it. If you are interested in it, first make sure it fits your goals and personality.

The military can be a great experience and an excellent opportunity for developing leadership, self-confidence, and management skills. However, it is not for everyone. If your goals coincide with military life, an academy or ROTC training provides excellent training and professional job experience.

I don't recommend the military route to financing education unless you want the military experience. The most favorable route is college first through an academy or ROTC, and then starting as an officer where you will have leadership and professional experience. The more intelligent you are, the less happy you are likely to be in the military unless you are in a position of leadership and authority. If this is your goal, then start with a college degree, not as a foot soldier. Creative, independent thinkers are often not happy in the military.

Entering the military as an enlistee or joining the Army Reserve in hopes of getting college paid for later is less likely to benefit your career path, and much more likely to have you driving a truck in the desert or laying in the dust, shooting a gun and being shot at. If this is not for you, don't do it. Military service is a life-altering experience for most people; for some it is good, for some not. Before making a decision, read about it, talk to people who have gone through it or are doing it.

Some people dream of success and; others wake up and work hard at it.

~Colin Powell

CHAPTER 13: CHOOSING A COLLEGE: THE HARVARD QUESTION

The greatest danger for most is not that our aim is too high and we miss it, but that our aim is too low and we reach it.

~Michelangelo

There are eight "Ivy League" universities; all in the Northeast U.S. Seven of these schools predate the American Revolution. The term "Ivy League" refers to football league, not academics. It was originally a derogatory term; these schools did not lower admission standards for athletes. As a result, these schools did not have as competitive teams compared to schools that lowered admission criteria to recruit high school athletes. Thus, they were 4th division teams, designated by the Roman numeral IV.

These eight universities have long histories and thus many successful graduates. Much of the prestige of the Ivy League schools dates back to times when they were exclusive schools for white men from wealthy families. In 1930's, Yale admitted over 70% of applicants, mostly from private schools, many of whom were legacy candidates. The prestige came not from the quality of education so much as the money these families had.

Although they once were the reserved of upper class, white, Anglo-Saxon, protestant men, they are now known, along with several other, mostly small and expensive private schools, for their highly selective admission criteria. These are prestige schools, as they are the most acclaimed and exclusive schools in the country. These schools attract, and selectively admit the brightest, hardest-working, most successful students from around the world, and as you might guess, their graduates often turn out to be bright, hardworking, and successful.

There are some distinct advantages to going to a highly selective, private university. These advantages, however, may not be the ones you'd expect.

Should you apply to highly selective colleges? Let's assume that you are the smartest, hardest-working, and most creative thinker in your high school. In that case, you should go to the best college to take advantage of your sizable intellectual gifts, drive, and passion for excellence. Obviously, you should apply to Harvard.

Reality Check: While you may be the absolute apex of intellect at your institute, astute, articulate, and accomplished acolytes abound among the millions of students graduating high school each year. Just for a moment, imagine that instead you are apt and assiduous, and egocentric. If your ego is not just big, but extremely inflated, then go ahead and apply to Harvard. If you get in, you will be in similar company there: a whole village of individuals with oversized egos, assuring each other how great they are in an expensive city with a miserable climate. If you relish cut-throat competition, cold, wet winters, and people who luxuriate in self-admiration, Harvard, a decent school, maybe just the place for you. (If your blood is boiling and you are red in the face, please relax; I am mostly joking.)

About 3.2 million high school diplomas are awarded each year in the U.S. If you are in the top one percent, you are one of 32,000. There are about 37,000 high schools in the United States, and 37,000 kids who graduate first in their class and you may be the one on top. Harvard has seats for 1,655 freshmen but accepts about 2,000, as some students will go elsewhere. Some students come from outside of the United States. Is it possible to gain admission? For the fall of 2012, Harvard accepted 5.9% of its applicants, about one in 17. For 2012, Yale accepted 1,975 students (6.8%); Princeton, 2,095 students (7.9%); and Columbia accepted 2,363 students (7.4%). Thus, Harvard and the other Ivy League schools don't have enough space for all the exceptionally bright kids, and competition gets tougher each year.

The odds, however, are good for a lottery for which the prize is worth winning. If you're in the top few percent of your class (for most schools), follow the advice in this book to get an ACT score of 33 or above, and you should have a decent chance of being admitted to an Ivy League school. The real question is whether Harvard, or another prestige school, is the best fit for you for your undergraduate education.

I submit for your consideration that Harvard does not hold a patent on outstanding undergraduate educational practices, does not guarantee you a successful career, and that there are 100 other colleges where you may be happier, learn more, have more opportunity to stand out and impress people, and have more fun.

Graduate education is a horse of a different color; not just for a great education, but for the connections. A Harvard law degree can open doors to major law firms (however, those firms may also be among those where it is most difficult to get promotions). It may be worth noting that Barack Obama and Mitt Romney both have Harvard Law degrees, but Rutherford Hayes was the only other Harvard Law graduate to make it to the White House. (Trivia: twelve U.S. presidents have attended various law schools – only seven of earned law degrees.)

While several Harvard undergraduates have gone on to be the president of the United States, this occurred mostly when there were only a few universities available. Both Adams, both Roosevelts, and Kennedy were Harvard graduates. Princeton can claim Madison and Wilson, and Yale graduated Taft and both Bushes. Four College of William and Mary graduates became President of the U.S., but none in the last 170 years.

Your college alma mater is not going to make or break your political career, or probably make or break any career. An MBA from Princeton can help with business networking – especially if you know how to schmooze with the aristocrats. However, don't expect it to work unless you show up at Princeton knowing the language of the upper crust, dressing and playing the part, and driving the right car. Moreover, you may not want to play the role if it is not whom you want to be. Graduating from these schools, especially at the graduate level, can open doors. What you do once inside those doors is the most important thing.

If your goal is making business connections, a Princeton or Harvard MBA is a great resource. If you want to work in finance, a Dartmouth degree is a great asset. If your plan is to be a corporate CEO, a Princeton business master's degree will likely help, but going to one of the top public state universities is just as good or a better way of getting into the US Congress, Senate, or governor's mansion for that state. If you want a corporate CEO position, gaining overseas business experience will be more important than the name of the school on your diploma.

Econometric studies show that paying for high-priced Ivy League tuition does not pay off for most students in terms of lifetime income. Students who must obtain loans to pay for going to these schools end up with more school debt and do not earn a high enough income differential over their career to make up for the extra costs. Top schools also don't guarantee highest salaries. However, there is income advantage in attending one of the top 100 public colleges in the country, rather than lower ranked colleges, especially if you can get the lower in-state resident tuition. If you are accepted into an Ivy League or another top-ranked private school with a free ride, however, take the opportunity!

Within a few years of graduating and starting work, your baccalaureate college will make little difference. What will matter is what you learned, how well you learned to solve problems, and what career you enter.

If you go into a medical field, it will not matter much where you got a nursing degree, as long as you are certified. You will earn the same income as a medical doctor if your undergraduate degree is from a state university or from M.I.T. Even the medical school attended makes little difference unless you want to do academic research, in which case you will earn less than most doctors in practice. In medicine, the difference in income comes from the specialty; surgeons typically earn several times more than pediatricians do. Engineering graduates earn far more than those who major in early childhood education or sociology.

The field you choose has much more impact on income than where you go to school. A degree in Art History from Stanford may help you get the museum job, but it will still be a low-paying profession. Income, and even finding a job depends on supply and demand. Currently, there are over a thousand graduates with Ph.D.'s in philosophy applying to every faculty position opening.

Rather than choosing a college based on its historic fame, choose a college on its value today. There are schools that are only a few years old, but are great colleges. Find a school that fits your interest and your personality. Find a place that you will be happy. Attend a school that will not bankrupt your family. Even if you have ample educational savings, you may want to conserve as much as possible for graduate school.

- Find a school that you can afford, so that you don't run out of money half way through. You don't want your education to end midway through because you overspent on a fancy name.
- Look for a school where you can thrive academically. If you impress your professors, it can open up opportunities and enhanced your prospects of getting into a graduate school and into the profession of your choice. Graduate programs have become increasingly competitive. You will need to be competitive to get into one of these programs, and you can benefit from the accolades of professors you impressed. This may be harder to achieve as an undergraduate at Columbia than at Mid State U.
- Look for a school, often a school in your own or a neighboring state, where you qualify for the in-state resident tuition, and which is in the top 100 public schools in the country.

Even if you plan to go somewhere out-of-state to put distance between you and your parents, you should apply to at least one in-state school as a back-up plan in case you aren't admitted to one of your top choice schools, or don't receive a financial aid package sufficient to make it affordable for you and your folks.

•   Apply to schools where you think you will be happy. Investigate student ratings of colleges to see where and why students are happier as certain schools. The reason for happiness should align with your goals.

•   Avoid schools where the graduation rate is low.

•   Seriously consider a STEM degree (Science, Technology, Engineering, and Math). Graduates in psychology, art, literature, education, and journalism, on average, earn half the lifetime income of those with a STEM college degree. Even if your goal is to be a journalist, a degree in economics or in physics can be a more useful asset to a journalist than a degree in journalism. If you plan to be an artist or musician, do these as minors.

•   Consider a smaller school. Small schools often have much smaller classes that give a better education with more interaction between faculty and students. Smaller colleges often concentrate on teaching undergraduate students, rather than on graduate students and research.

•   Don't go to a party school if you are a party animal, or are not self-disciplined. There may be too many opportunities for fun and risk, and too many distractions that keep you from learning and graduating.

•   Avoid schools where your only choice is to reside in a 3 or 4-person dorm room. With one roommate, you can negotiate, and control your environment. With more people in the room, you will be at the mercy of the crowd and their worst behaviors. If you are obtaining a STEM degree, you don't want to be stuck with roommates majoring in libation and copulation, who want to use the room to party when you need to study or sleep.

•   If you want the prestige of an Ivy League diploma, you will get more for you money by waiting and earning their master's or doctoral diploma than an undergraduate diploma.

Do these famous "Ivy League" schools and other selective and highly rated private schools (Stanford, University of Chicago, Colgate, Cornell, Duke and many others) provide a better education? This is hard to tell. They start out with exceptionally bright, talented, hard-working, overachievers. Those same overachievers would almost certainly do well in life if they had attended any good school. There is no question that there are prestige and bragging rights associated with these famous schools.

In a few years, it is likely that there will be testing of college graduates in different fields, similar to the Bar exam for lawyers or medical board exams. At that point, we may be able to get an idea of which schools do the best job of educating their students, or at least which are best at picking the best students.

For now, try to pick a school with a reputation for satisfied students, with a high graduation rate, and a school that fits you. Look for schools with smaller classes and one that focuses on teaching undergraduates, not just on research.

Smaller Class Size: There are advantages to schools with smaller class sizes where the professor actually teaches the class. In many large universities, during the first two years of college the introductory classes are taught by a graduate student in huge lecture halls filled with 600 or more students. In most large, research-oriented universities, your lecturer may be a graduate student who has never taught before. The best graduate students are working on exciting research; teaching assignments usually go to the weaker graduate students, often a foreigner with poor English language skills. If you don't understand something, you don't have the opportunity to stop the lecture to ask questions. Among the highest ranked colleges, are small liberal art colleges, such as Swarthmore, that don't even offer advanced degrees.

Smaller classes, filled with bright students, provide opportunity for higher-level discussions and learning. They allow for Socratic teaching and inquiry, foster intellectual development and logical thinking, rather than having students sit, as a passive audience.

There are advantages to going to smaller schools, even those that don't have out-sized reputations. Check out the student: faculty ratio of schools where you are thinking of applying. Students tend to rank small schools the highest for happiness. Some large schools have small class sizes and are taught by real professors. Do your research before deciding.

Engineering undergraduate students tend to be at the bottom of the heap when it comes to student happiness. They often are dissatisfied with the teaching and the quality of their professors. Nationwide, engineering schools have very low graduation rates; 40 to 45% is typical. Some engineering schools, however, stand out among the very best schools for student satisfaction and graduation rates. These are small, private colleges such as Harvey Mudd College, Franklin W. Olin College of Engineering, and California Institute of Technology, all of whom pride themselves on their student happiness and graduation rates that average over 75%. These programs focus on undergraduate education and hands-on experience. These schools also provide generous financial aid and have their pick the most diligent students, which helps explain their success.

If you are interested in applying to a larger university, find out if they have an honors program that you might be eligible for. The honors program can surround you with other bright, motivated students, and give you access to exceptional opportunities. The honors program can replicate many of the advantages of an exclusive, small college within a larger university. Some schools have an honors dorm, where you can actually study, get some sleep in, and make friends with the brightest new students on campus.

The prestige of a university is often based more on fame and the number of students it has graduated than on anything else. Of course, that makes it well known. A university that has been around since the Declaration of Independence or which graduates 10,000 students a year is expected to be well known and have many famous and successful graduates. That does not make the students or teaching any better.

Some schools try to impress by faking how exclusive they are. They advertise heavily to high school students through glossy direct mail and social media to increase the number of applicants. Their ads show attractive young men and women having fun on campus and playing sports, or traveling to vacation sites in Europe and the South Seas. The school is presented as if it were a Club Med holiday resort for young people. They then use the revenue from the applications to pay for more advertising. The goal is to increase the number of applicants, in large part, so they can say that they only accept a small percent. The lower the percentage of applicants they accept, the higher they can hold their noses in the air, the more they can charge for tuition. Some schools raise their tuition, just to look more exclusive, and then give partial "scholarships" to entice students.

Among the universities with the lowest admission rates, are California State University – East Bay (22%) and California State University - San Bernardino (19%). These two California state universities are not highly selective private schools, but state universities serving areas with a large population of candidates. The College of the Ozarks admits only ten percent of its applicants; however, this may be a result of providing free tuition to all its students; thus, giving it the same admission rate as M.I.T.

Attracting students that are more competitive makes a college look better. It is easy to have smart graduates if a school fills up with students that were their high school valedictorians. It does not necessarily follow, however, that the education provided is better, or that it would be better for you.

The most salient reasons for selecting a highly selective private college are *happiness and low costs!* Look for a college where you will thrive and be happy. The Princeton Review of colleges and other guides reveal a correlation between how selective a college's admission standards are, how happy its students are, and how likely their starting students are to graduate. However, if you are accepted to a highly selective college but don't belong there and are struggling academically to keep up, you will likely be miserable. Success feels great; floundering is awful.

A second factor that influences satisfaction with a college is size. Many of the schools that score highest in student satisfaction are smaller and cater to undergraduate students. The most dissatisfied, unhappy college students are those in commercial, open-enrollment, for-profit, chain schools such as DeVries. (www.collegedata.com) These are also some of the schools with the worst grade inflation and lowest graduation rates.

A third factor that seems to be associated with student satisfaction is diversity. Schools with more regional, ethnic, and cultural diversity are happiest. Perhaps this is because those students chose to be there, rather than choosing a school because it was conveniently close to home.

A fourth factor in student happiness seems to be if the school is a private college. Engineering students are notoriously dissatisfied with their educational experience. It's a tough row to hoe. I screened data from www.collegedata.com for engineering schools with a 75% or better graduation rate and an 85% or better satisfaction rate. Only seventy-one schools of 626 private and public colleges offering engineering degrees met these criteria. Sixty-three of these were private colleges, four were U.S. military academies, and the four other public, four-year colleges were University of California Berkeley, University of Virginia, University of Michigan, and the College of New Jersey.

Another factor is academic selectivity. Almost all of the colleges where students rated their freshman year as very happy were very selective schools. It may be that very selective students (bright, energized, and dedicated) are happier with the college experience wherever they go. It may be that these students that are performing well, are less stressed about grades, and have less financial worries than the average public college student.

The Princeton Review of Colleges rates happiness by different metrics, including the quality of campus cuisine and number of sunshiny days. When you do your research, remember to look at the factors important to you. Your selection criterion for schools should include where you will believe you will happy and thrive. Look at the ratings for happiness in the Princeton Review of Colleges, or look online to for colleges you are considering. You want to do well, enjoy the learning experience, and graduate.

Affordability: Many of the Ivy League schools have been around for a long time and have had many successful graduates. Many private schools are not only good at finding qualified students, they also are good at raising money, or may be similar to Stanford, which was started with a large endowment gift. Many of these schools have huge financial endowments. A few years ago, Senators Grassley and Baucus nudged these schools to utilize tax-free endowments to help students from lower income families or risk losing their tax-exempt status. This helps level the playing field and increase student diversity at these schools.

Many of the top private schools in the country have generous financial aid for middle and lower income students. Harvard, Stanford, M.I.T, and many other elite private schools pay most, if not the entire educational cost for lower and middle-income students, including housing costs. Some schools also provide merit financial aid to students with high GPA's and high placement test scores. Thus, if you are accepted to some of the top colleges in the country, you may not need to worry about how to pay for your education. It is almost as if a scholarship was part of the acceptance package. These schools complain that they don't get enough applications from gifted low-income students to use the monies they set aside. If you want to attend one of these schools, and have a decent shot at being accepted, you should apply. It might cost you less to go to a private school than to attend a state college. If you are from a low-income household, you may be eligible for an application cost waiver. Even applying may be free.

Investigate the cost you would pay to attend private schools that you are interested in. You might be surprised how affordable they may be for you, especially if you are from a low or middle-income family. www.Collegedata.com and similar websites have data on which colleges will help with tuition and housing costs. If accepted, Harvard *will pick up the entire tab*, including housing and meal tickets if your family income is under $65,000, or use a sliding scale maxing out at 10% of income for families earning under $150,000[2]. Even that $15,000 is well less than the cost of attending a public university. Even those from upper-income families may get help. Elite private colleges can be bargains for those with great grades and placement test scores.

Every college is required to have a "net cost calculator" on their website that gives an estimate of what it will cost a student, based on family resources, to attend a school. You may be surprised that for middle or lower income families, your cost may be less than at a public university. Google "net cost calculator" with the name of the school you are interested in to find what it will cost to attend that school, before deciding to, or not to, apply. The www.collegeboard.org website also has data for net cost for most colleges but requires the student to log in.

Many of the selective private universities 90 to 100 percent full free tuition and on-campus housing to students from low-income families, and generous sliding financial aid assistance for middle-income families. There are over 60 private selective colleges that provide 100% financial aid to lower income students, including:

- Brown University
- Cal Tech
- Columbia University
- Cornell University
- Duke University
- Rice University
- Harvey Mudd

- M.I.T.
- Stanford University
- Swarthmore College
- Princeton
- Vanderbilt University
- Harvard
- Yale University

Some top ranked U.S. colleges provide free tuition to all of their students regardless of family income. These include:

- Curtis Institute of Music
- Web Institute (Engineering)
- Deep Springs College
- Macaulay Honors College

U.S. Military Academies:
- (Army) West Point
- (Navy) Annapolis
- Air Force Academy
- Coast Guard Academy
- Merchant Marine Academy

A list of the very generous colleges that provide 100% financial aid to students from middle and lower income families is provided on the supplemental information website (See Appendix A). These schools are quite competitive. The list also includes some other generous private colleges that while not quite as generous, may provide over 90% support to middle and lower income students, Among these are some colleges that are only moderately competitive.

Graduation: The highly selective schools usually have high graduation rates; in most of the elite schools 85% or more of the students graduate within four years. However, some schools don't. Georgia Institute of Technology only has a four-year graduation rate of 31%, and Kettering University's is only 11%! When you are young and feel invincible, having never failed anything, you may believe it could not happen to you. However, if half the students that start a program don't finish, please don't assume you will be immune. If it is that hard to survive, how much fun can it be? Investigate why the failure rate is so high. In some schools, many students need more time, which means it costs more to graduate.

Before choosing your college, make sure to pick one where you have the best chance of success. This is especially true if you are in a high-risk group for not graduating: minority status, attending a high school from which most students don't attend college, if no one in your family has a college degree, or lower social economic status. If you are in these any of these groups, choose a school that excels in the area of high graduation rates, not one that prides itself on weeding out weak students.

Some of the common reasons students fail to graduate from college include:

1.   They were not academically ready for college. This occurs mostly in schools that do not use a high enough ACT or SAT score for filtering out unprepared students. I don't believe setting up students for failure is generous or even ethical. It would be better for these students to start at a community college that focuses on getting students ready for higher-level studies. An ACT score of 22 is considered the threshold for college readiness. For more rigorous degree programs, such as engineering or nursing, a minimum score of 25 is more appropriate.

2.   Running out of money. It is not just tuition. Food, clothing, rent, cell phone, transportation, books, and pizza all add up. Plan ahead so that you will be able to finish before you go bust and need to get a job.

3.   Partying. Alcohol and drugs do not support academic achievement. If you have a proclivity to imbibe, you may do better at a "stone cold sober" college. (A list is published in the annual Princeton Review of Colleges.) You will still need 9 hours of sleep when you are in college to have your brain function optimally.

4.   Lack of Self-Discipline. There will be many distractions, and your mom will likely not be there to remind you that you need your sleep, to get you up in the morning for class, or to do your homework.

5.   Playing cowboy. Going it alone is more common for men and minorities. Loners do poorly. It helps to study with friends, share notes, commiserate of the difficulty, and work as a team.

6.   Pregnancy. It can be avoided. Condoms and birth control are available, usually without cost, from most student health centers and health departments.

Check out websites such as www.collegedata.com, www.collegeprowler.com, or the "U.S. News" site on colleges.

These websites have information on:
- Acceptance criteria of colleges
- The financial aid amount you can expect according to your family's income,
- Satisfaction indices of freshmen for different schools, and
- Graduation rates for different schools.

Consider too, that different majors at these schools may have different success rates. You can call the universities you will be applying to, and ask them what their graduation rate is for students in the field you plan to study.

NOTE ON COLLEGE SATISFACTION: I have a friend whose son was miserable at Cal Tech and I know a woman who experienced hell at Harvard, two schools highly-ranked schools by the Princeton Review for student happiness. Just as it is difficult to determine if the teaching is any better at the highly selective schools than at state schools, there is little way to tell if private colleges are happier places. When you don't have stress from excessive academic burden, financial stress, or feel physically threatened, when you have free time to relax, get enough sleep, and have a good social network and a bright future, you are much more likely to be happy. If a private school can provide a safe, nurturing environment, relatively free of worry – that should be a setting for academic bliss. Then again, if you are free of worry because you are easily passing your classes, and have no financial woes because of adequate scholarships and financial aid, you may be happy almost anywhere, especially, if you are surrounded by upbeat, happy souls. Smaller classes allow you interact more, and get to know more people than do darkened lecture halls.

Wherever you end up, surround yourself with bright, exuberant, engaging people. You may need to put aside your reticent nature to introduce yourself and make friends. These friends can be your social network now and professional network in the future. Having friends who focus on their education and on making a better world will help you do the same. Friends, a sense of community, and freedom from worry help cultivate happiness and success. Hang out with winners and you will probably be one. Hang out with whiners, and you will do that, too.

You can never cross the ocean unless you have the courage to lose sight of the shore.

~Christopher Columbus

CHAPTER 14: TAMING TEST ANXIETY

Many of our fears are tissue-paper thin, and a single courageous step would carry us clear through them.

~Brendan Francis

Those who suffer from test anxiety may know the material and have great, creative minds, but still do poorly on tests. They may thus be excluded from great educational opportunities.

There is a secret to overcoming the deleterious effects of test anxiety as well as other forms of anxiety: accept it. Don't try to avoid the anxiety, as that empowers it. *Fighting anxiety feeds it.* Just let it be. It is okay to be anxious. If you take time to understand your enemies, they will often no longer be your enemy. This holds true for anxiety.

Anxiety is your brain telling you something. What test anxiety is telling you is that the test is important. You knew that, didn't you? It's not a surprise? So, thank the non-verbal, right side of your brain for reminding you of that.

As you are walking out the door of your house, do you ever have the feeling you forget something? This is the right side of the brain hinting, "Something is amiss" or at least saying "Please review the 'leaving the house' checklist." The verbal, left side of your brain then says something like, "Stove off, have wallet, lights turned off, have keys, bathroom visit..." After reviewing your list, you determine that everything's cool, and you take off. Your mind is at ease again.

Anxiety is less pleasant, and hopefully reserved for more unusual events, but it is analogous to what occurs when you are about to leave your house. It is an alert to check your environment for danger. It is not a confirmation of danger; just as the sense of missing something when you leave the house does not mean that you left the stove on.

Anxiety is only a feeling. It's there to inform you of a potentially dangerous or urgent situation that needs your attention. The right side of the brain deals with emotional content, but is not much good with ideas, content, or words; these are the prerogatives of the left side of the brain. The right brain only knows that an alert has been triggered by something in your environment – it is a general alarm signal. It does not indicate imminent danger or a crisis requiring you to escape. The alarm is telling you that a sensor has been triggered. Often, this occurs when a situation reminds that brain area of a similar occurrence where there was stress or danger.

It's nice to have a dog that lets you know when a stranger enters your yard. It's annoying to have a dog that barks all night long, barking at crickets or leaves moving in the breeze, or barking because it hears another dog yapping a mile away. If you have a dog with a nervous or excitable disposition, it may bark at all kinds of things that are of no consequence. That is what test anxiety is. So pet your dog, saying, "It's okay, puppy, there is nothing to worry about," and in a few minutes the anxiety will settle down.

If you fight anxiety, try to control, or dominate it, it will often get worse. Your brain is telling you to watch out; if you ignore it, it will just increase the volume of the alarm and yell louder: "OH NO!!! WATCH OUT!!!" Trying to suppress the alarm distracts your attention from your task, making the test more difficult.

It is better to acknowledge the anxiety so it knows it has done its job: "Yes, I'm taking a test, it's important to me. That's why I'm anxious."

Perhaps a long-forgotten childhood experience has affected me. Whenever I was at the dentist's office and the dentist walked in,

I'd panic. I'd be trembling inside, breaking into a cold sweat. I had to fight the overwhelming urge to bolt from the office. I sometimes stopped the dentist mid-procedure to let my agitation abate. I'd leave dents in the dentist's chair from grasping the seat in white-knuckled terror. I would leave, chilled from my cold sweat, embarrassed by what must have appeared to be cowardice.

I don't hate dentists. I was even engaged to one. Nonetheless, I have dental procedure anxiety. It has been severe enough to motivate scrupulous dental hygiene and flossing, which allowed me to evade the dentist chair for more than a decade. Then, a thirty-year-old filling failed; I had little choice but to face my fear.

As a child, I suffered from severe cynophobia. So, I would run away from dogs. Dogs' instinctual reaction is to chase, and often to bite. So, I got bitten on several occasions, each time reinforced my fear. It was time to stop running, time to learn to tame the beast.

An anxiety response still is triggered when I visit the dentist. However, I have learned to accept my anxiety reaction as part of my dental visit, and I don't worry about it anymore. It's just information my brain gives me, and I look around and think, "Yep, here I am in the dentist office and that makes me anxious." After a minute, I relax and let the dentist do the procedure. No sweats, no chills, no terror.

Accept anxiety as information that is presented to you. Anxiety and fear are temporary feelings that will pass. These emotions may be triggered by an association with an event that occurred long ago in your past, and have no significance to your current situation. Every time the smoke detector goes off, it does not mean your house is on fire. Look to see what is causing the alarm to activate before running, screaming, from the building. The purpose of these emotions is to let you know there may be danger or that a situation warrants action. The right brain is asking for a risk assessment; give it one. Assess the situation and make a decision about how to proceed. If you do not get upset about the alarm going off, and review your checklist to identify the alarm trigger, if any, the alarm will usually quit within a couple of minutes. Your anxiety will diminish each time you approach it this way.

If you feel anxious during a test, acknowledge it. Tell the brain, yes, it's another test. Look at how it makes you feel, but realize it will abate in a couple of minutes, like a noisy car next to you at a stop light. In a minute or two, it will be gone.

Enhance your cool – do the Victory Dance!

This exercise has been scientifically documented to lower distress hormone response and improve performance during stressful situations. When you are about to enter a difficult test, have a job interview, meet new people, or walk into other stressful situations, you can boost your confidence and decrease your reaction to stress by tricking your brain into a calm confidence.

Throw your arms into the air in a huge victory V, as athletes do, bounce on your toes and smile broadly, looking back and forth as if smiling up to an admiring crowd. Perform the victory dance for 90 – 120 seconds, in the minutes before your stress situation. You may want to hide out in a bathroom to perform this dance, or perhaps gather a crowd of friends and share the trick, depending on the situation.

You can then enter the situation feeling more relaxed and confident.

It ain't no use putting up your umbrella till it rains!

~ Alice Caldwell Rice

Chapter 15: Your Curriculum Vitae

What a man thinks of himself, that is which determines his fate.
~Henry David Thoreau

A Curriculum Vitae (CV) and a résumé are different creatures. A CV is longer, detailed, and may never be seen by anyone other than its writer. The résumé is a summary, which is adapted for each particular job, school, or scholarship application.

Having a well-prepared CV will make the application process for college and scholarships easier, less stressful, and more successful. If you do not have one ready, I can almost guarantee that when it comes time to fill out college applications, you will forget activities and accolades that you would have wanted to include in your bio but missed during the frenzy to completing your applications on time. You can avoid considerable stress in as deadlines approach, simply cutting and pasting the activities, honors, and awards from your CV into your application.

If you do not have a CV, start one today. However, don't expect to complete it anytime soon. This document develops with you and needs to be revised and appended periodically. Add to it whenever you have a new accomplishments or activities.

Use the CV as a personal log to keep a record of dates and details of your accomplishments, including work experience, community and volunteer service, extracurricular activities, honors, and awards. Volunteering one Saturday to clean a park may seem too trivial to mention, but when you have a dozen events over 3 years, it becomes a picture of who you are. It is no longer 4 hours, but rather 48 hours of community service. Keep the names and contact information of adults you work with, so that you can get in touch with them in the future if you need to.

Your high school CV should include accomplishments and activities starting from the summer prior to your ninth grade. High school level work, sports and honors accomplished during the 8th grade may be included if the activity continues into high school.

Curriculum Vitae	Résumé
The CV is a comprehensive accounting of your accomplishments. It may contain details, such as the name and contact information of your supervisor or teacher, time spent, dates, and other details.	A résumé is a brief synopsis to get you in the door. You have 20 seconds to make a good first impression; this is your chance. Your goal is to get into the list of candidates being considered.
The CV includes awards and accomplishments, volunteer and athletic activities, and educational achievements. It is used primarily to maintain a record for yourself, but also used in academic situations, for internships, scholarships, and fellowships.	The résumé is adapted to the specific position of interest. Expect to revise it every time you send it out, adapting it to the focus on the particular position you want to be considered for.
There is no page limit to the CV. If a CV is submitted, it should be revised to be polished, well written, and limited to pertinent information.	The résumé should be polished and to the point. It should be a single page (at most two pages), easy to read, and attractively formatted.

In your CV, include the number of hours per week and weeks in a year you participated in an activity. Write a couple of lines (20-30 word) describing of the activity and its accomplishments. List the dates or time-period when the activity or accomplishment took place. In contrast, when you prepare your résumé, think of it as a series of Tweets, in which you need to pack detail and elicit interest, but only have a limited number of characters available. You need to be brief and succinct, and carry across your identity.

Most private colleges and universities use the Common App (CCA) form to apply to their school. The following résumé format is designed to make it easy, when the time comes, to transfer the data from your résumé to the application.

The CCA provides space for five *Honors or Awards* related to academic achievements beginning ninth grade. For each of these 100 characters are allowed, including spaces. The CCA also gives space for up to ten *Extracurricular Activities*. Fifty characters are allowed to identify each activity, plus 150 characters, including spaces to describe the activity. Provide as much descriptive information as possible within the character limits.

TIP: To count characters in MS Word, hold down the left mouse button, and mouse over to highlight the area. Click on the *Review* tab, and then on *Word Count* in the proofing area to see *Characters (with spaces)*.

Additionally the CCA asks for the number of hours per week, weeks per year, and class years you participated in the activities you report. Be sure to keep this information in your CV, even if you do not include it on your résumé. You can include more items on your C.V. or résumé, and then select the ones you are proudest of to include into the CCA. Avoid repeating the same items even though it may fall under both headings.

Your educational résumé should also include a brief description of your career goals and desired college major on your résumé. It is okay if you are interested in many areas and have not yet decided, but at least put down some areas of interest, perhaps a "social responsibility interests" if you have any. For example, "A professional degree in an applied science and management, that will prepare me to help resolve problems in the area of minority education," or as per your interests; health, environmental issues, social justice, etc. Undecided is not a bad college major.

Model High School Résumé Contents:

Full Name
Mailing Address
Phone Number and Email Address

- Name of high school, city, and expected graduation date
- Class ranking (if in top 10 percent) and GPA (if above 3.0)
- Best ACT or SAT composite scores
- College and AP courses

Honors: Include academic honors and awards you received from the 9th grade on. While this area is mostly for academic achievements, if you are applying as a musician or athlete, awards in these areas can be described here. Include competitive summer programs. Limit these to 100 characters. Include honor societies only if you have nothing else to fill up five slots.

Extracurricular Activities: These help tell the story of who you are, what you value, and what interests you. These activities help set you apart from other applicants, and help create a sense of person for the reviewer. The listing of the number of hours of involvement per week and weeks per year, and the years you were involved is not required on a résumé, but needed for the CCA.

- Summer programs and internships
- Community service, volunteer, and leadership activities
- Work experience: Even if the job is not a great one, holding a job shows responsibility and reliability, and willingness to work with and for others. If the earnings go to college savings or support your family, say so.
- Athletics: Participating in athletics shows that you are a doer and gives an aura of vitality. You don't need trophies or championships, however, if you have them, list them.
- Other extracurricular activities (including hobbies): accomplishments, publications, presentations, and performances.

Kevin B. Dansing
123 Parish St., Midland, Iowa, 46205
Mobile Phone (901) 555-5438
Kevin.Dansing@email.com

EDUCATION:
Eagle Rock High School. Expected Graduation: June 2015
GPA: 3.78 (Unweighted)
Class Rank: 41 out of 534
AP Courses: Language, Literature, Chemistry, Physics
ACT Score: 32

HONORS AND AWARDS:
- AP Scholar with Honor Award
- National Society of High School Scholars Academic Paper Award
- Cellist at the All-State Music Festival on the campus of Iowa State University, 2013 and 2014
- Herbert Hoover Uncommon Student Award; Secured use of 44 walls for outdoor public art murals
- Mu Alpha Theta Mathematics Honor Society –participated in regional math competitions, 2014, 2015

WORK EXPERIENCE:

• *Midtown Public Library; Assistant*
Checked in and shelved returned books. Read to groups of small children. Assisted patrons in finding reference materials and using computers. Summer of 2013 20 hours/week, 8 weeks.

• *"Computer Nerds" repair shop; Assistant Technician*
As a summer job, I repaired and upgraded both software and hardware problems at a computer shop, testing, diagnosing problems, eliminating malware. Summer 2014. 34 hours/week, 10 weeks.

• *Gear-Heads Community Bike Shop; Volunteer*
Volunteer apprentice mechanic and instructor; teach and assist other bicyclist to maintain and repair their bikes using donated and recycled parts. Year Round 2013-14, two hours/week.

MUSIC:

• *"Cat Gut Chamber Orchestra"; Cellist*
Perform charity and fund-raising events in an elite classical chamber ensemble. Only eight of 170 symphonic music students are accepted into "Guts". 2013-15, 32 weeks/year, 3 hours/week.

• *Band leader and songwriter for "Sage Grouse"*
Perform and record indie-pop compositions, as vocalist, guitarist and cellist on pieces I have written or collaborated on with other musicians. Year-round, 3 hours/week, 2011-2015.

EXTRACURRICULAR ACTIVITIES AND HOBBIES:

• *Eagle Rock High Robotics and Programming Club*
Weekly lunchtime club. We designed and built a robotic window opener/closer, acting on outdoor temperature or rain, based on an Aduino module. 2014, 30 weeks, 1 hour/week.

• *Eagle Rock High Culture Club – Vice President*
Help organize and prepare a weekly event with ethnically themed meals and music. My specialty is bison, and Native American dishes and music. 2012-14 30 weeks, 1.5 hours a week.

• *Iowa Prairie Grass Native Plant Society: Member*
Interest in mycology and foraging for wild edible plants. Habitat restoration volunteer; waist deep removal of aquatic invasive species. Member since 2010-14. Monthly meetings and events.

• *Sunshine pastimes and other athletic pursuits:* I enjoy non-competitive athletics including catamaran sailing, ballroom dancing, bicycling, unicycling, and juggling. Year-round, 2-3 hours /week.

• *Personal Challenge Accomplished:* Canoed the 46-mile Current River in the Ozark Mountains over a five-day primitive camping trip during the summer of 2014 with a friend.

EDUCATIONAL GOALS: A professional degree in biomedical engineering. I hope to develop improved prosthetics to help enable injured patients, such as those injured from land mines to regain mobility and function.

Listing induction into honor societies as an honor adds little to a college application. They already know your GPA. If you actively participated in an honor society, describe your activities as an extracurricular activity, telling what you did. Only use these as filler if you don't have other awards. Even then, try to use your 100 characters to say what you did.

Tell the truth. Don't invent or claim awards not received or activities not done. Don't exaggerate, but neither hide your accomplishments. If you don't tell scholarship boards or admission committees of your activities, they will not know. If you got an 18, a 24 and a 29 on three different tries at the ACT, report only your best score. If you won a church baking contest for your chocolate chip cookies, you can say that you won a prize for cooking. You do not have to elaborate. And, while honesty is essential, this is not the time or place to air your dirty laundry, shortcomings, weaknesses, disabilities, or make excuses.

If you have enough material to make your résumé two pages, do so. Do not stuff your résumé with trivial events or activities as this makes it appear that you have nothing of substance to include and gives the impression that you lack focus and commitment. It is better to squeeze a CV into one page than to fluff it into two.

TIP: If you have dabbled in several activities, and your résumé appears to lack continuity, find commonalities in your activities, group them under headings and place them in an order that ties them into unifying themes. If you read to children in the library, were a tutored math, and coached soccer, you might list these all under the heading of "Youth Leadership." If you played in a band, were in a school play and enjoy tap dancing, these could be listed under the heading "Performing Arts."

An inclination for mountain and rock climbing may not seem something that a university or scholarship board would be interested in. Such activities, however, show that you are a doer.

Playing computer games and watching television rarely merits a scholarship. Producing videos or creating computer games does. Involvement in more unusual activities (sculling, sailing, scuba diving) may get more notice than marching band or basketball, unless you are expecting to participate in these activities in college. Sky diving or bungee jumping may be considered too high risk, unless you are trying to get into paratrooper school but this may not be helpful for more conservative colleges.

Transformational experiences that affected your life can be impressive – however, these experiences will not be taken into consideration if you don't disclose them. You need to articulate your accomplishments on your résumé and in your applications. Especially with activities, use action words that describe what your role was in the activity, what you accomplished, enjoyed, learned or provided to others.

Household responsibilities, such as unpaid babysitting, or chauffeuring siblings to games or great-grandma to the doctor can take up time, that you might have used for activities to adorn your résumé. Don't fret; even when it is not voluntary and not paid, it is still work experience; even if you enjoy doing it.

• *In-home caretaker for elderly woman:*
Assist my great-aunt with cleaning, laundry, meal preparation. Drive her to doctor visits; monitor medicines and vital signs; provide companionship. Ten hours weekly, 2013-14.

Including this in a resume will earn a lot more respect than being VP of the Culture Club. If you mow lawns and trim hedges, it is landscape work. Look up job descriptions for what you already do, and see what activities and duties you do that you can list. Taking out the garbage and making breakfast, however, neither makes you a sanitation engineer, nor short order chef.

Common high school activities (marching band, junior varsity basketball, cheerleading, theater productions), are more impress if your team is state champion, but unless you were the goat, most individuals playing team sports have little impact on winning championships; they are a team efforts with coaching making a huge difference. Being on a winning team does not certify your greatness, being on a losing team does not make you a schmoe. Including these activities shows your love of sports and willingness to work in a team. Even better is to accept leadership and organizational when they open to you.

Selective colleges seek candidates that have shown dedication to interests beyond the high school curriculum. Extracurricular activities include, but are not limited to sports. Your activities and accomplishments can reveal initiative, leadership, persistence, and independent thinking, and integrity. It is being able to lead yourself and work with others to accomplish goals.

- Persistence is shown by extracurricular activities that continue or evolve over several years, not just sampling.
- Initiative is shown when you start something new, or set out on your own to do things outside of what is offered as part of regular high school activities.
- Integrity is shown by conviction to ideals rather than to short-term personal desires.

SPOILER ALERT: When describing your goals on a college or scholarship application, résumé, or interview, be specific and modest in your goals. We all want to save the world. Focusing on an area where you may be able to make a small, specific, tangible improvement will show maturity and understanding of the enormity of how difficult changing the world is. Ending hunger and world peace are platitudes suited best to Miss America.

When compiling your list of activities and accomplishments, describe the activity as actions. Show that you are a doer. Avoid using the verb "to be" your résumé; don't be; do. Try to avoid redundancy by using a variety of action verbs.

Verbs to Describe Activities

Achieved
Ascertained
Adapted
Administered
Advised
Analyzed
Appraised
Approved
Assembled
Audited
Authored
Broadcast
Budgeted
Built
Calculated
Catalogued
Choreographed
Clarified
Communicated
Compared
Compiled
Composed
Computed
Conducted
Constructed
Consulted
Controlled
Coordinated
Corresponded
Created
Delegated
Demonstrated
Derived
Designed
Developed
Devised
Directed
Discovered
Earned
Edited
Eliminated
Enhanced
Established

Estimated
Evaluated
Examined
Facilitated
Filmed
Financed
Formed
Founded
Generated
Governed
Guided
Identified
Illustrated
Implemented
Increased
Inspected
Installed
Instilled
Integrated
Interpreted
Interviewed
Introduced
Invented
Investigated
Launched
Lectured
Led
Maintained
Managed
Marketed
Mastered
Measured
Mediated
Modeled
Moderated
Monitored
Motivated
Negotiated
Organized
Originated
Performed

Persuaded
Planned
Prepared
Presented
Prioritized
Produced
Programmed
Promoted
Proposed
Proved
Provided
Publicized
Published
Recommended
Recycled
Reduced
Regulated
Rehabilitated
Reorganized
Repaired
Researched
Resolved
Reviewed
Revolutionized
Rewrote
Scheduled
Screened
Served
Simplified
Solved
Started
Strengthened
Succeeded
Supervised
Systematized
Taught
Tutored
Trained
Translated
Upgraded
Verified
Videographed
Wrote

Window Dressing

Things to Leave Off Your Résumé

• If your G.P.A. is less than ideal, leave it off your résumé.
• If your class rank is lower than the ideal, leave it off. For highly selective schools, you need to be in the top 10 percent or your class. You are not required to give your class rank on the CCA.
• Short term employment that could give the impression you didn't last or keep a job. Any job you were fired from.

Cell Phone Message

Call your cell phone and listen to your message. Your councilor or the program you are applying to may call you. The message you made two years ago and forgot, which may have seemed funny or cute, may come across very differently to stodgy, old adults who don't know you or have your sense of irony. Include your name and make sure your articulation is clear so that you sound educated. It may take several tries to get a recording right.

It may help to write down your message and read it. Here is a script for a sample message you might consider:

You have reached (first and last name)'s phone. I am presently unable to take your call. Please leave your name, number, and reason for the call. I hope to return your call shortly.

Facebook Page

Log out of your account and look to see what the public sees on your Facebook page. Make certain that pictures of you skinny dipping, jumping off bridges, osculating or snogging are hidden from the public, or even better, never posted. Since Facebook keeps things forever and puts them on a timeline, if you have been indiscrete in your postings, it may be advisable to close your Facebook page and create a new one that presents you as an up up-and-coming professional. Colleges, universities, employers, and scholarship board members may look at Facebook pages to see who you are, and to help them decide if you are what they are looking for. Use Facebook to create the image that you want to project. Use a photograph that makes you look good, not something goofy on your profile.

Leave snarky, rude, racist, sexist, small-minded, angry, cynical or mean comments off your page. You are better than that. Don't say anything about anyone that you would not say to their face. When you are outraged by something, let your angst simmer and cool before making a reply that may not reflect well on you, or may hurt someone you don't mean to offend.

Consider how your post might appear to people you may need help from to move forward in the world. Remember, as unfortunate as it may seem, it will be mostly adults who control your access to success in life. You need them on your side.

Email Address

If you have an email address name that no longer reflects how you wish to be perceived, at least by universities or scholarship boards, it may be time to create a new one. Boozer@party.com deviltrash@atheist.com, or Hotty16@hotmail.com may not portray an image that helps with scholarships or admission to the college of your choice. Even if only used for applications, get an email address that imparts a professional appearance.

You can make a free email address using your first and last name at Hotmail, Yahoo, or Gmail. Mail.com has hundreds of free email tags, such as *atheist.com, hiphop.com,* and *engineer.com.* Avoid these. Stick to mundane ones such as mail.com or email.com. Even using *engineer.com* may be seen as being presumptuous if you have not yet enrolled in that area.

Google Yourself

Look for your name, with your city, and see what comes up. If it is not complementary or is misleading, you can have Google remove it from showing up in their search. If you are a minor (under 18), most infringements can be sealed in public records.

Always be a first-rate version of yourself, instead of a second-rate version of somebody else.

~Judy Garland

Don't limit yourself. Many people limit themselves to what they think they can do. You can go as far as your mind lets you. What you believe, remember, you can achieve.

~Mary Kay Ash

CHAPTER 16: LEADERSHIP 101

The task of leadership is not to put greatness into humanity, but to elicit it, for the greatness is already there.

~John Buchan

Colleges are always on the lookout for leaders. Top colleges understand the importance of leadership in achieving success in life, so they look for leadership in your application. How does one manifest leadership? Winning an election for president of the chess club? Being the most popular and charismatic kid on campus? Being a boss who tells people what to do? Starting your own business? Wielding power over others? Sorry, none of these things is leadership.

Being a successful manager requires getting people to work together to accomplish a task. Tyrants do not need to be leaders. They intimidate their subjects, coercing them to do their bidding through threats, fear, and intimidation. Leaders act differently. They inspire people to work together to accomplish a goal. The diagram below is used to help explain leadership:

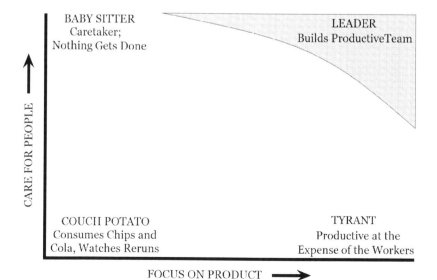

I was a physician in a county in Florida with a single high school where a new, young, football coach was hired. He had big goals. His plan was not to remain teaching at a small high school making $30,000 a year, but to be a college coach, or even better, to be a professional team coach where he could earn ten times as much. His plan was to have his teams win tournaments, proving his abilities so that he could move up in the ranks.

Football practice started in early August and he trained his players hard. It was hot, in the high 90's with near 100% humidity, nearly every day. After two players with injuries and two with heat exhaustion came into my office over several days, I called the school and raised hell. This guy cared only for production that would make him look good, and nothing about the players he was using to tread his way to the top. Like most selfish acts, it was also shortsighted. Most of the players quit or were injured before the season even began, so that he didn't even have enough players to build a team. Tyrants care little about the lives destroyed building a monument to themselves, but this only works when there is an endless supply of slaves to exploit.

A babysitter, in contrast, cares for children, but nothing gets accomplished. An example is a substitute teacher showing movies in class, but who does not teach. A country club atmosphere at work is fun, but there won't be paychecks for long if the company has no income. Couch potatoes are bosses who don't care about people or production. Everyone's time and resources are wasted.

The diagram shows a shaded triangular area to illustrate that some of the time, taking care of team members has a higher priority than producing the highest possible results, whether those are producing widgets on a factory floor, teaching children to read, or producing a musical. There are other times that a leader asks team members to make sacrifices, such as to work overtime to meet production requirements or prepare for an event. Flexibility and adaptability are essential qualities for leadership.

Leadership includes:

- Forming a shared, motivating purpose
- Building a team spirit and sense of identity
- Developing trust and protecting team members from harm
- Producing actions that lead to progress and results
- Motivating individuals, instilling enthusiasm
- Helping team members develop new skills
- Selecting members with various talents for specific tasks
- Ensuring that team members share in the rewards
- Solving problems

A good leader outlines clear goals and makes those goals exciting and achievable. This may mean breaking goals down into simple steps. Leaders motivate their team, enticing them with the prospects of achieving their mutual goals. Enthusiasm is contagious and leaders develop enthusiasm in their team through their excitement.

Leaders build a team and eliciting members' enthusiasm to work together. Building a group identity helps develop team cohesion and spirit. Uniforms and emblems show group identity. Something as simple as t-shirts, caps, or a pin with a team insignia can help create a sense of team identity.

Leaders pull a plan together. A consensually developed plan, combining and selecting the best ideas of team members to achieve the goals is best. Leaders build consensus and keep the group focused on developing the plan; help negotiates disparate interests, and keep the team on task to achieve the goal.

Leaders build cohesive teams that will be effective. They build camaraderie within the team and promote a shared sense of identity. This does not require a top-down management technique.

It does not require a managerial position as a supervisor, boss, president, or officer to be a leader. A team member provides leadership when they perform the function of a leader by building excitement and cohesion within their group. Leaders build trust between team members. Likewise, a boss or team member can be an "anti-leader" by undermining cohesiveness with favoritism, jealousy, small mindedness, selfishness, or by spreading malicious gossip about other team members.

The philosopher Lao-Tzu said that the best leader is invisible.

When the best leader's work is done the people say, "We did it ourselves!"
                                                                      ~Lao-Tzu

Good leaders adapt to the situation and to the members of the team they lead. Different individuals bring different skills, abilities, and baggage. Some days, a member may not be at their best, and the leader must both act on behalf of that team member as well as the other members of the team. Genuine concern and compassion are traits of a leader. Leaders adapt to circumstances and changes direction as the environment changes to produce the desired product. Goals and plans need to evolve and be modified to complete a mission. A great leader maintains an evolving consensus.

Leaders create an environment that builds friendships and trust between team members, and prevents jealousy, animosity, or suspicion, which can disrupt team cohesion. A leader makes team members feel that their contributions are appreciated and important. It is not a team if the members are not working towards a common goal. Members should learn from each other, and while each member is important, no member should be indispensable. If you lose one member and the goal cannot be achieved, failure will ensue.

Leaders protect the team members from harm, both physical and emotional. Members will perform more effectively when they trust the leader to protect them and act in their interests. Team members should feel that they are treated fairly in comparison to other members, are rewarded with opportunity, and compensated fairly for their contributions. A great leader strives for every team member to have a positive experience, resulting in growth in their self-confidence and self-esteem, and acquiring skills.

Everyone has strengths and weaknesses; leaders identify these. They help members develop their talents and skills, and direct these talents to achieve the team goals. Leaders are aware of weaknesses members have, and create opportunities for individuals to overcome those deficits. This is what good coaches do. They provide mentoring and build self-confidence in team members. A leader ensures that team members have the opportunity, tools, resources, and authority they require to succeed. Good leaders never pile on responsibility without ensuring that the resources required for success are available.

Finally, all team members should be rewarded for the success of the team. Some members may contribute more and be rewarded accordingly. Every member of the team should be rewarded fairly. Leaders assure that each member feels they have been.

Leaders bring out the best in us. In a partnership, including relationships such as marriage, both individuals should be leaders, bringing out the best in each other. Truly great leaders transform their team members into leaders.

If you have done these things, even without a title, you are a leader. If you have acted to build cohesion and camaraderie in a group, helped motivate others to achieve, helped formulate and achieve goals, you have been a leader. In your résumé, essays, or interviews remember that if you have acted as a leader, you are one. Leadership is not limited to a single individual at the top of an organizational chart. You can use the vocabulary describing leadership in this chapter to describe situations where you have shown leadership. The word "leader" need never appear.

Leadership at one time meant muscles, but today it means getting along with people.

~Mahatma Gandhi

What can you do it you are stuck in low-achieving high school; perhaps a school too small to have challenging classes or one populated with apathetic teachers and classmates? BYOL: be your own leader. Ask your language teacher for books that stretch your level that broadens your perspectives. Take on-line or dual enrollment classes especially for math and sciences. Spend some of the time you would be studying at a more competitive school preparing to get a great ACT test score, and be prepared to do make-up learning when you get to college.

If you are in a weak environment, rather than tuning out, take advantage of the vacuum and become a leader. There may be little competition for positions that provide public speaking and leadership experience. Being the big frog in a little pond has its advantages. It is not by chance that Truman, Eisenhower, Johnson, Nixon, Carter, Reagan, and Clinton were all from small towns. Rather than competing with many great students, as you might in larger or higher performing schools, you may have many opportunities to stand out, develop people-skills and self-confidence, and earn accolades for your activities.

Leadership is solving problems. The day soldiers stop bringing you their problems is the day you have stopped leading them. They have either lost confidence that you can help or concluded you do not care. Either case is a failure of leadership.

~Colin Powell

CHAPTER 17: TAMING THE APPLICATION NIGHTMARE

I love deadlines; I love the whishing noise they make as they go by.
~Douglas Adams

Der frühe Vogel fängt den Wurm. (Early birds catch the worms)
~Proverb

I know you just love the image of fat red wigglers being pulled out of the dew-covered turf, and being sucked down by robins on spring mornings. Nevertheless, it is true. There are only certain times when the opportunity presents itself. The most important step for getting into a great college is applying, and getting it done on time. This also applies to applications for financial aid.

Completing college applications and getting them in before the deadline can be the most stressful process many high school students have endured. Numerous students have meltdowns and throw in the towel on their first choice of colleges when they see how much work it is, how small their chances seem, and how little time they have left. Other students compile their application in a last minute, "Hail Mary pass" attempt, with little likelihood of success for winning scholarships or gaining admittance to a selective college. The stakes are high, leading to stress behaviors that further lower the chance of success.

If you are tempted to take the last-minute approach, as many of your classmates will, consider the last three years of work you have put into school: the time you spent studying for classes, preparing for tests. Think about any boring volunteer work or extracurricular activities you might have done, against my sage advice, just so that you might look good on an application. Do you really want to do a slipshod job in the final stretch?

Highly selective schools get 15 or more applications for every seat available but don't let this dissuade you from applying to a school you are in the running for and want to attend.

Firstly, many of the students applying to top-tier private colleges are "reaching" for schools they don't have a GPA or placement test scores high enough to even be considered. Numerous students (in need further instruction in statistics) apply to 20 different schools thinking that if they have a 5% chance in each, it will assure their entrance into at least one competitive school. Thus, the ratio of *qualified applicants* to the number of seats available in these highly competitive schools is much lower than 15:1, likely closer to 5:1.

I can run a mile in about six minutes. I can try this every day, and on some days, I may be able to run a mile in five minutes and 40 seconds. There is never a day, no matter how many times I run, that I do a four-minute mile. The main effect of students submitting inadequate applications to multiple schools, hoping to get lucky, is to lower admission rate numbers. Submitting applications that don't make the cut to more schools does not raise a student's chances of getting into a competitive school.

Don't let the depressingly low admission rates dissuade you from applying to the school or schools of your choice. Check the 25 – 75% GPA and test scores of students attending the school. If your GPA and placement test scores are above the lower 25% of those gaining admission to the school, your chances are excellent.

Secondly, qualified applicants often apply, to and are accepted into multiple schools, but can only attend one. This too, inflates the number of applicants to the number of seats available; making it look harder to get into a school than it actually is.

Thirdly, and perhaps most relevant: high school seniors, even highly intelligent and accomplished ones, often are not prepared for the application process. Let this serve to your advantage;

avoid the time trap most students fall into. A large majority of students submit last minute applications. Most of the students you will be competing with, for a seat at that elite university, will complete their essays and applications in the final 24 hours. Their applications usually show this haste. Don't make this tactical error.

Last minute applications are so common that university and scholarship application websites have often crashed in the hours before the deadline, making it impossible to complete or upload applications during those final hours.

NOTE: When your friends find themselves locked out of application sites the night of the deadline, and they are freaking out, reassure them: most colleges want the applications. If their server has locked-up, the college will usually extend their deadline; sometimes only for an hour past midnight, sometimes for a day. Encourage your friends, letting them know they will probably be able to get their applications in, if they keep trying.

A rare instance where it is beneficial to lie to yourself, it is to tell yourself that the deadline is weeks earlier than the actual date and hour. Set your application calendar ahead by two weeks, and plan to get your applications in three weeks early. You probably won't, but at least you will be ahead of the game

Avoid the stress by starting early and planning. Creating a great application, which differentiates you from the deadliners, may be the best secret of getting into a great school and winning scholarships. Expect to put in 30 to 40 hours of work over a two-month period. Begin before the first day of your senior year.

Preparing Your Application

Imagine for a moment that you are an admissions officer. The computer has already deselected applicants with scores too low to be considered, unless flagged by the dean. You are now tasked to select several hundred students out of many thousand qualified applicants with great GPA's and placement test scores.

You might look to see if the application:

- Reflects a person who cared enough to spell correctly and use proper English.
- Showed passion for learning.
- Revealed a personality through their essays.
- Did not seem too fragile to withstand much stress.
- Seems to be friendly and accommodating enough that they will not be likely to strangle their roommate late some night.

If you had to pick from among several qualified applicants, why not pick someone who is nice to be around, that has a sense of humor, appears honest and enthusiastic, is comfortable communicating their feelings, shows persistence and calm in the face of adversity, and plays well with others? Canned, bland, or rushed applications can rarely reveal these attributes.

It is reasonable to optimistically apply to a school you would love to attend that is a bit of a reach with a great application, but a waste of time to send out a sloppy application to multiple schools you have little chance at getting into.

College Applications

There are three paths to apply to individual colleges: apply directly to the college, use the Universal College Application, (UCA), or use the Common College Application (CCA). Most state (public) colleges have their own applications, usually online.

UCA: Despite the name, the UCA is not universally used. At the time of this writing, it is employed by only 44 schools, and most of these schools also use the CCA. Thus, there is little reason to use this form unless it is the only form used by the school. Many schools require supplemental information along with the UCA.

CCA: About 500 colleges and universities use the Common College Application, including most well known private colleges and universities. Unlike the UCA, the CCA requires an essay (for almost all schools) and letters of recommendation. Some of the schools that use the CCA require submission of supplemental materials. The advantage of using the CCA is that it reduces time and redundancy when completing applications to multiple schools and allows you to focus on doing one application with great care. There is no fee for completing the CCA; however, the individual schools usually charge application fees.

The CCA is available at www.commonapp.org.

Colleges that participate in the either the CCA or UCA programs must pledge that they will not give preference to applicants who use the school's application. An advantage to colleges using the CCA or UCA is that it makes it easier for students to apply, who might not otherwise do so (as it can be as easy as checking an extra box). This is a marketing tool for these schools; it increases the number of applicants, and thus makes the school appear more desirable and more exclusive when they turn away more students. It also makes money for schools that charge application fees.

ALERT: Be aware, many schools include additional material to customize the CCA application. Perhaps they do this to help prevent applications from non-committed applicants.

Visit the admission web page of schools you are interested in to see what application options are open for your top choice schools. Read about their specific applications. The school's website may also give you clues regarding what they are looking for in applicants, letters of recommendation, and art supplements.

Early Admission

Your best chance of getting into your first choice school is often through early admission. This process usually has a deadline around, and far more frightening than, Halloween. In the first round, competitive schools may give admission for more than half their available seats to a much smaller number of early applicants than will apply for regular admission. Some colleges and universities now skip the early admission and have a regular application deadline as early as October 15 or November 30. QuestBridge match applications are due in late September of the student's senior year! This means that students who are interested in early applications need to move forward on their applications by September 1 to have time to complete a polished application that presents them at their best. Better yet, begin your application preparation in August. Be prepared to put 40 hours into preparing a polished application.

There are two main forms of Early Admission; some colleges offer Early Action; others Early Decision:

- Early Decision is usually restrictive and binding; if admitted you are committed to going to that school.
- Early Action lets you know you have a spot, but gives you the option to shop around and decide later, depending upon scholarship money or other factors.

Early Admission allows prospective students to apply to a single private college and receive notification of acceptance (or not) as early as December 15th. Students are allowed to apply to only one private school through Early Admission. If they found to have applied to more than one, they can lose their place at any of the schools. Students who apply for Early Admission are free to apply to public colleges, regardless of the application dates. Some private schools, such as Vanderbilt actually have two early decision dates.

Tip: Early Admission application may greatly increase your chances of admission to certain universities. Harvard accepts fewer than four percent of students who apply in the spring, but accepts 19% of early admission applications[5]! Many elite private colleges have higher admission rates during the Early-Admission round.

Other schools, Yale, for example, say that its early action plan does not raise the chances for admission into their school; rather, a higher percentage of early applicants meet their application criteria. Schools with a higher "Early Admit Ratio" give greater advantage to students who apply during the early round.

University	Early Admission Rate[6]	Regular Application Rate	Early Admit Ratio
Dartmouth	25.5%	10.8%	2.36
Cornell	36.7%	15.5%	2.37
Brown	23.7%	9.5%	2.49
Yale	13.4%	5.2%	2.58
Columbia	22.5%	8.2%	2.74
Princeton	21.1%	6.7%	3.15
Harvard	18.9%	3.6%	5.25

A benefit of early application is that if accepted early in your senior year, you will have that huge concern out of the way. You can then focus on all the myriad of other things you have in your life! If you remain undecided at the end of October which private universities is your first choise, you might choose one with the non-binding early action. If you get accepted, you are in, but can still make other choices.

Once you have selected the school you have been accepted to, you should let the other schools you have applied to, and especially accepted to, know that you have chosen to attend elsewhere. This lets another student have a chance to attend in the spot you would have occupied.

The Application Process

1. Start early. What would you do if you found out that three additional essays are required for the Stanford application supplement at 9 PM the night of the deadline? The chances of getting into that school drop tremendously. Do your homework and find out what is required and desired with plenty of time.

Check out the deadlines for the schools you are interested in during the summer before your senior year. For early application, the deadline is November 1 for most colleges. Some public colleges have application deadlines in September and October.

The QuestBridge match application deadline is in September, around the 25th, depending on the year. This program helps lower bright, high-performing students from middle and lower income families attend one of the top private colleges, without cost. The student lists their top three school choices in an extra-early admission process. The median income for a family of four in the United States is about $54,000. Students from families with annual income under $60,000 are eligible for this program.

2. Read the colleges' undergraduate admission website page. Each school may have particular information that gives clues as to what they are looking for in students, and may have specific information on their application process. This is especially important for students applying as musicians, other artists, or as athletes. Some schools, such as Princeton, required SAT subject tests. You will need to know this so that you can take the tests in time to have the results ready for your application.

3. Art and Music Supplements: Many schools accept or require an art supplement or auditions for dance, theater, music or art majors. Artists and performers may want to submit art supplements, even if they are not majoring in their art. Remember, that Harvey Mudd and Stanford, even though great engineering schools, consider themselves to be liberal arts

colleges. Even if you don't plan to major in an art, a supplement that shows exceptional talent may enhance your chances of admission to the school.

If you plan to submit an art supplement, the deadline may be even earlier than the early application. For musicians, dancers or other performers, and audition may need to be scheduled months in advance, and the art supplement turned in weeks ahead of the application deadline. Check the school's admission website.

Many schools request a pre-audition audio or video recording of the musician or singer, soloing. Make sure you have time to prepare it.

4. Update your CV (see Chapter 15) and have it ready. This essential task will prevent stress and help you recall all the great things you have done over the last few years. It will make it simple to cut and paste sections on extracurricular activities, honors, and volunteer work from your CV into your applications. Having it ready ahead of time allows you to present yourself as a more three-dimensional individual within the two-dimensional page. Your extracurricular activities can show you as a multifaceted, committed, caring individual, with leadership experience. While you complete your applications, update your CV as you think of improved wording for descriptions of your activities or remember other activities you may have left out.

5. View the application process as a test. Students that prepare for tests generally do better than those who walk into the classroom not remembering that a test was scheduled.

6. Select from among the colleges you have considered, and pick your top private school choice for early application. You only get one "early admission" opportunity and only one choice.

Among your applications, include at least one back-up college choice. This should be a college that you are confident you can gain admissions to and one that is affordable. This might be an in-state public school. You can begin submitting applications for regular admission as soon as the early admission deadline passes.

7. Meet with your high school counselor before school starts your senior year and request a copy of your transcript so that you have a list of your classes, GPA, and class ranking. Make sure that you have received the proper credit for the classes you have taken and that any omissions or errors are corrected. Check to make assure that any classes you may have taken off campus are recorded on your transcript properly.

Let your counselor know which colleges you plan to apply to. Make sure you have the required classes for those colleges, and register to take any SAT subject tests that may be required. Keep in mind that your counselor will write your evaluation. It's a good time to be pleasant. Provide them with a copy of your CV, and ask them to go over it with you. Make sure that your counselor is aware of your extracurricular and volunteer activities.

8. By the first week of September, you should have a Common Application account online if you are interested in attending a private college. Start filling out the demographic data; this is the easy stuff; your name and identifying characteristics, parents and contact information.

Read through the entire application, taking notes, so that you can begin working on it offline, and contemplate ideas for the essays. Download the applications for your other college choices. Make sure your CV contains all information needed for the application questions.

After asking for a letter of recommendation, and on the day you enter and assign the person in the common application, send an email to your recommender, letting them know that they should watch for an email from the Common App, and that you appreciate their help. Especially for your school counselor, attach a copy of your resume, even if they have seen it before. This will help them remember all the activities you participated in while in their school.

> WARNING! The deadline for submission of letters of recommendation is the same day as it is for the application.
>
> At least three weeks before your application deadline, you need to ask three people; your high school counselor and two teachers, for letters of recommendation. After they agree, you need to put their names and email addresses into the online Common App. After entering their names and email addresses, make sure that they are "assigned". The application will show them as assigned only if the entry is activated and successfully sent. The Common App organization then emails instructions to these persons.
>
> Since the deadline for letters is the same as the application, if you wait until just before the deadline to assign your recommenders, *they will not receive their email invitation until it's too late* for them to get it done! Furthermore, imagine that 20 other students may ask for letters from the same teachers just before the deadline. What personalized accolades can you expect in such moments? Last minute request for recommendations from a teacher or counselor may put them into a bind, which they may resent.
>
> Allowing sufficient notification time for the recommender to write your letter is perhaps even more important if you are getting a letter of recommendation from an extracurricular recommender, such as an employer, coach, or supervisor at the soup kitchen where you volunteer, that is not familiar with the process and deadlines.
>
> You do not need to submit the Common App before your recommenders get notified. Notices are sent as soon as you activate their names within the CCA online application.

Letters of recommendation for the Common App should not be specific to any school that you may be applying to as the same letters will go to all the schools you apply to using the CCA.

WARNING!!!: *You only get one chance to make a first impression.*

And, you only get one chance at the CCA. Once you submit Common App, *you will not be able to alter it when applying to another college.* (You may get one edit of your essay) You will only be able to append it with updated grade reports as you complete classes.

Your letters of recommendation, your activities and honors are the ones you submit the first time around. This same application, thus, goes to every school the CCA goes to. Your early admission application will have the same data as your regular admission applications. Make sure your Common App reflects you at your best when you submit it! Rushing through, to complete the Common App the night of your first early application deadline, may not serve you well.

Do not peg your Common App to one school. If you mention your lifelong dream of attending Princeton, it may dissuade your secondary choice schools from accepting you.

If you've submitted a hideously botched Common App, and want to apply to a different school, some private colleges allow you to use their proprietary application form or the Universal App. Most of the schools that use the CCA, however, only use the CCA.

Once you have a Common Application account, you will be able to select the colleges you want to apply to and download the supplemental forms that may be needed for various schools. Many colleges request some additional information; many require an additional essay or other materials. Don't wait until the deadline to find out.

Most state schools have their own applications. Make sure to look through them with plenty of time to make sure you will have time to complete them, and complete them with due care.

8. Save your work. Create a new folder on your computer to save your essays, application forms, and other files. This will make it easier to find them later. As you save them, number the essay files sequentially so that you know which one is the newest and correct version, as there may be several revisions. Create a second folder for the older editions of your essays and move these older ones there to avoid confusion when copying or uploading your essays.

By October 1, you should have most of the information for your applications saved online in the forms. Be careful to save your work periodically, as some online forms timeout after a period of inactivity, causing you to lose your work. Keep a copy of your application information. For PC's: type "Control-A" to select all, right mouse click, "copy", and then paste the application into a word document to save it for later use. By October 1, you should also have made headway on your essays.

9. Get the essays polished. Reread the essay prompts to make sure you are answering the prompt appropriately. Use different required essays to highlight different aspects of your personality. The Common App extracurricular essay is a great place to highlight leadership experience (see Chapter 8).

By October 7, your essays should have been reviewed by your most erudite mentor after having been rewritten several times. Read it aloud to make sure it flows well. You need to let your essays rest a few days between readings to do them justice when reviewing them.

10. Submit your applications a week early. In 2012, Hurricane Sandy knocked out power to millions of people for a week, the night before many applications were due. Computers crash, the

internet goes down. Life happens. Leave yourself a margin of safety.

11. You may want to supplement your application with a phone call to the admission office, especially if you have not had an opportunity to visit the school. Use this call to ask questions about the school and the program to show your interest, and with follow-up with emails, so they become familiar with your name.

If you have the opportunity, a visit to the school is even better. Clicking an extra box and paying an extra $90 to apply to an extra school with the Common App does not demonstrate much interest. It is just an expensive lottery ticket, if you don't let the school personally know that you want to go to their school.

I skate to where the puck is going to be, not where it has been.
~Wayne Gretzky

Application Questions

If a school asks about your favorite music, movies, newspapers or books, they are trying to get an idea of your interests and of who you are. Eclectic tastes in media suggest an individual open to new experiences, who loves to explore, and who thinks independently. Most schools hope to attract a mix of unique individuals to build their student body.

If you are asked about your favorite book, "Harry Potter" is not the ideal answer. First, you will not stand out from thousands of other applicants. Also, remember that *"Harry Potter and the Sorcerer's Stone"* was written at a 5th-grade reading level. If you list a book from a series, be specific, and tell which of the books your favorite is. If you are asked about your favorite magazine, remember that you might want to list an on-line magazine.

APPLICATION FEE WAIVERS FOR LOWER-INCOME STUDENTS: If you have taken the ACT or the SAT, and are from a lower-income family, these organizations will provide an application fee waiver for three colleges each. Ask you guidance counselor. You will need to supply the Fax number for the college admission office to your counselor at the time you apply. Many colleges also have independent fee waiver programs for lower income families.

ADVICE: Do not let your parent complete your college application, even though they may volunteer to unburden you with their help. Their words will not sound like a high school student's words. The reviewer will likely realize that it was not a high school student completing the application. The student needs to complete this process.

Parents, however, can help their kids considerably, aiding in the organization, encouragement, and patient support through this stressful process. Parents can prepare a tag list, and calendar for items that the student needs to get ready: deadlines for applications, updating the CV, getting their transcript, and keeping essays moving forward. Parents may be able to proofread essays, and if time permits give hints as to where they can strengthen their essays.

A truly courageous, and dearly loved parent, may help, much to your chagrin, by telling you when your essay is not the genius work you believe it to be. They may suggest that you write about something you care about so that passion comes through in your essay.

The CCA asks for some information that the applicant is not required to answer. These include class rank, test scores, graduation date, ages of siblings, parent's email addresses, demographics, family income and if the applicant has children. Most schools do not use this data to discriminate, but rather to plan for financial aid, and for increase diversity. If you are applying to a college that is *not* highly competitive, and your test scores and class rank would impede your chances of admission, you might want to leave them off.

The CCA has an "Additional Information" section. Even though this section is optional, it can be a valuable area. The applicant can write about anything they want added to their application. This is the one area of the CCA that can be modified as many times as needed, and can be modified to go to one school if applying one school at a time.

This area is sometimes used to explain situations outside of the student's control that negatively impacted their school performance. These may include prolonged illness, injury or homelessness that the student experienced during high school. Also, it can be used to describe special situations that you feel the college should know to better evaluate your promise as a student.

If used to talk about impediments, including low scores, grades, or disciplinary issues, use it to explain how you overcame setbacks or learned from the experience, rather than as a place make excuses or beg for pity.

This section may also be used to expand on areas that other spaces seem too limited to reveal individual and their strengths. It might be for a second essay on extra-curricular activity, community service, or to shine light on achievements.

NOTICE: In the days following your application, you will likely get emails to confirm your application and asking for missing or additional information. If you do not, check your junk mail folder. You will have only a few days to complete any missing or additional info requested.

ALERT: Be aware that included in these emails for early admission applicants, may be a request for completing financial aid applications, also due within a few days. The forms, the FAFSA and CSS, are discussed in the following chapter. In these, the family income for the previous year is needed for the FAFSA, and estimates for the current year are needed for the CSS, along with information on currently held financial asset values. Since the assets and income usually belong to the student's parents; a parent usually needs to be involved in this process, which can take several hours.

Students not participating in early admission should also be aware that they should file the FAFSA every year for which they plan to attend college, even if they have not yet filled out their college applications.

A critical step in gaining admission into a great college or winning scholarships is applying, and getting a well-prepared application in on time. This also applies to applications for financial aid. Most financial aid, including that from the state and federal government, is in limited supply, and those who apply late can lose out.

A goal is a dream with a deadline.

~Napoleon Hill

Action is the foundational key to all success.

~Pablo Picasso

Chapter 18: Financial Aid Applications

Whoever is careless with the truth in small matters cannot be trusted with important matters.

~Albert Einstein

Most of the money available for college does not come from merit-based scholarships, but rather from need-based financial aid. About $7.5 billion is distributed as scholarships annually; meanwhile, there is $150 billion in need-based financial aid given each year. Need-based financial aid will introduce you to a new form of alphabet soup with acronyms such as SAR, CSS, EFC, EOCG, and others.

In the United States, need-based financial aid can be divided into two categories, government aid, and private sources, mostly from the university the student attends. Governmental financial aid is awarded through use of the FAFSA application. Most private aid is applied for through the CSS application.

The FAFSA Application

The FAFSA is the aptly named Free Application for Federal Student Aid. Student attending over 5,500 public and private colleges and universities in the United States are eligible to receive federal financial aid. Almost all state colleges and universities use this application for students to determine financial aid eligibility. The FAFSA is additionally used by over 600 state financial aid programs and for many private scholarships and school programs. Even if attending a private college, students need to complete the FAFSA application to receive financial aid for those colleges.

To be eligible for federal financial aid, the student must be a US citizen or legal resident of the United States. The FAFSA application can be completed online (www.fafsa.ed.gov) and it is free. This application must be completed for eligibility for federal financial aid programs, including Pell Grants, SEOG, Stafford loans, and Perkins loans.

Federal Financial Aid Programs:

- **Pell Grant:** Grant to students with financial needs for undergraduate education. The maximum grant is about $5,500 per year.
- **SEOG:** Federal Supplemental Educational Opportunity Grant: Provides need-based grants to low-income undergraduate students. The money goes to the school and is then doled out among their eligible students. The maximum grant is about $4,000 per year.
- **Perkins Loans:** A need-based loan that does not accrue interest while the individual is a student. The limit is about $5,500 per year with a maximum of $27,500 for undergrads and $8,000 per year and $60,000 maximum for graduate students. Loans can be forgiven in part for those who volunteer in the Peace Corps and those who teach in low-income schools or teacher-shortage subjects. The interest rate is set to 5%.
- **Stafford Loans:** A low-interest loan that does not have to be paid on as long as the student is attending college at least half time. If subsidized (for lower income students), the interest is paid by the government as long as the student qualifies as a student. For these students, the interest rate is 3.5%. For unsubsidized loans, the rate is 6.8%.
- **Federal Work-Study Program:** A federally funded grant to schools to provide part-time work to students with financial need, often in student's area of study. These jobs can be great opportunities for gaining practical experience in areas that otherwise are hard to break into.

For the FAFSA, the following documents are needed:

- The Social Security Number
- A driver's license (if the student has one)
- Documents for income: Tax returns for the previous two years (an estimate for the prior year can be used until the tax return is ready) and W-2 forms or other records of income. These will be the parent's or guardian's tax return and W-2 forms, unless the student is married, a parent, or over 24.
- Information on assets: Accounts, business or farm information, investments, mortgages, property value.
- Alien Registration card if not a U.S. citizen.
- Selective Service Registration if male and over 18.

Note: Currently, the best time to apply is January or February but beginning in 2016, applications will be available in October for the following school year. Reapply as early as possible each year you will be attending college the coming fall. Federal and other grants are in limited supply and funds usually run out. Early applications may increases the chances of being awarded financial aid.

A FAFSA personal identification logon (FSA ID) is needed and can be obtained at by visiting https://fsaid.ed.gov. If you have the old PIN number you can convert it to an FSA ID on this website. Keep this FSA ID login safe as it can be used to access sensitive financial information.

After applying, the student will receive an **SAR** (Student Aid Report) by email or snail mail if you don't provide an email address. Email is faster. This gives the opportunity to recheck the data that has been submitted and correct any errors that may have been made. There are about 100 questions, so mistakes can easily occur. A single mistake may make a student ineligible, so diligence is worthwhile. Schools and programs often require tax returns or other documents. The SAR data is sent to colleges that the student selects on the FAFSA.

The SAR will give an **EFC**, an Estimated Family Contribution. This is the amount of money that the Department of Education calculates the student's parents should contribute towards the student's education. Many middle-class families have incomes and assets which prevent eligibility for federal grants and subsidized loans. *Apply anyway.* This application is used by most states, many schools, and scholarship programs, and may help with other forms of financial aid, including Stafford Loans, which while not need-based, may come in handy. The U.S. Department of Education also has graduate educational funding programs for students working on master and doctoral degrees.

A video tutorial, "Seven Easy Steps to the FAFSA," provides helpful information on completing the FAFSA at: http://www.finaid.ucsb.edu/fafsasimplification/index.html

The Bottom Line: Even if you or your family have a very low income and receive the maximum $5,500 in Pell Grant, a $4,000 SEOG, and a $5,500 Perkins Loan, these combine only to $15,000 a year. That's $60,000 over four years. That is a very nice chunk of money. However, by itself, this is not enough to pay tuition at many colleges and universities, much less living expenses. Almost all students need additional funding. Federal financial aid should be thought of as a supplement for college funding and a source of moderately priced student loans.

Complete the FAFSA application as early as possible early to have the best chance of getting grants and work-study for the coming year. Apply during your senior year of high school, and then each year in which you will be attending college the next year. The application does not have to be completed in one sitting, but it is best to do it on one computer. For most students, the parents financial data will be needed, but the form can self populate much of the data directly from their IRS tax return.

Note: Every college is required to have a "Net Price Calculator" on their website. Use your data to see what that college will cost.

The CSS Application

The CSS application is a product of the College Board, the same company that makes the SAT and AP exams. CSS stands for College Scholarship Service although it not a scholarship application. About 650 mostly private colleges and universities use the CSS to determine eligibility for financial aid.

The CSS is not free; it costs about $9 for the application plus another $16 for each school or scholarship program it is sent to. This application only needs to be completed if applying to a private colleges or scholarships requiring this form. If you are worried about the cost of this application – then you certainly need to file it. This application may be your ticket to a free education at one of the top private colleges or universities.

The College Board provides low-income fee waivers to about nine percent of students who complete the CSS. The waiver is granted automatically, based upon on the financial information supplied. The CSS fee waiver allows eligible students to send data to up to six colleges or programs without incurring any cost.

The CSS is completed online, using the same account and password that the student uses for their SAT or AP tests. The application questions are adaptive, so questions an individual is asked, depend on answers to previous questions, and on the schools to which the student has requested information be sent. Most students will be asked about 70 to 150 questions. Link to the CSS: https://profileonline.collegeboard.org/prf/index.jsp

The CSS asks for more extensive financial detail than does the FAFSA. For example, the CSS asks for financial information from both parents and their spouses, even if the parents are divorced. It asks about home equity, business assets, and brokerage and retirement accounts. Normally, home value assessment for the CSS is capped at about 2.4 times the family's income.

Note: In the previous chapter, I advised parents not to meddle in writing their kid's college applications. In contrast, the parent should take the lead on completing the FAFSA, and especially for the CSS application, for dependent minors. The CSS asks for detailed financial information; including parent's bank account balances, investments, real estate holdings, and retirement accounts. Depending on the school, a copy of the parent's complete tax return or other documentation may be required. High school students usually do not have access to, and the parent may not want to provide their sons or daughters access to the financial data required for completing these applications.

While more intrusive, the private schools which provide financial aid are often much more generous than the Department of Education or state schools. The criteria for eligibility are often higher; meaning the students from middle-class families may be eligible for financial aid at many private schools when they would not be eligible through federal or state programs. The FAFSA defines income as *adjusted gross income* from line 37 on the 1040 tax form. The CSS asks details about total income and deductions and focuses on family wealth.

While the federal government sets the criteria for federal financial aid, the College Board just collects information and supplies it to the schools. Each school, or need-based scholarship program, makes decisions based on their own criteria. Some colleges will ask for additional information.

It is often helpful to speak with a private school's financial aid officer to discuss any special circumstances that may affect the family's ability to afford tuition and other educational costs. Some considerations, which may not show up on the form, might be medical conditions of a family member or financial burden from supporting family members outside of the country. The school's financial aid officer may have latitude in making decisions that help provide a student assistance.

The CSS asks about funds in retirement accounts. Colleges do not count these funds when making award determinations, except in unusual situations. It would be a mistake to assume that a student will not be eligible for financial aid if the parent has a fat retirement account. Stocks and other liquid investments held in regular accounts in the parent's names are assessed for the EFC at about 5% of their value. Savings and investments in the student's name are assessed for the EFC at 20% of their value.

When to apply: The CSS should also be completed early on. Some schools want the CSS for early decision applications and require it by November 15 of the year prior to entering college the following fall. Many schools require it by February 1st. Check the date required for the school or program you will be applying to on the College Board website by beginning the application form and adding the schools and programs to your list.

Normally, people do not even receive their tax documents for filing thier tax return until mid- to late-February, and some documents come later. High school students should alert their parent that financial aid applications need to be completed early in the year that they will graduate from high school, and that the parents will need to gather the tax and financial data required earlier than it is usually needed.

The CSS asks for income data even before the parent or guardian has earned it, making it difficult to give exact data when completing these applications. Thus, earning estimates are used, necessitating later refilling. The new change to October for FAFSA applications will use the penultimate tax year data for the next year's financial aid, making the FAFSA application much simpler; tax data filed with the IRS in April can be automatically inputted into the FAFSA in October of the same year. Hopefully, the CSS will follows the FAFSA lead on this.

Pittfalls: You can increase your chances of getting financial assistance by applying, accurately completing the application, and getting the application in promptly. Because of the early dates, most people will not have filed their taxes before the time when the applications are best submitted. For both the FAFSA and CSS, applicants are encouraged to use estimates of their income, and to submit the actual data as early as possible. Most need-based financial aid is in limited supply. While it is not first-come-first-served, the money available is limited and may run out before all eligible students get their applications completed.

At the time of this writing, one of the most common errors made in filling out financial aid applications is in assessing the value of the parent's home. Home values may have fallen in recent years. Parents who own homes should check Zillow.com or a similar source to see what similar houses in the area are selling for, before placing a monetary value on what many families consider their greatest financial asset.

It is not dishonest to pay debts, such as property taxes or insurance premiums and credit card bills that are due, prior to posting account balances, which the CSS asks you to report. Those liabilities already exist and thus, should be balanced against assets that you or your parents may have in assessing available wealth. While asking about assets, other than mortgages, the CSS does not ask about outstanding liabilities.

ALERT: Some may be tempted to hide assets or not honestly report income on the FAFSA and CSS. Be honest and encourage your parents to be honest about their wealth. Receive the aid for which you shall be eligible with gratitude; allow those needier than thou art to receive the need-based aid they merit.

If you are still tempted after my homily, then be aware that the federal government mandates that colleges audit, and require documentation for, a minimum of one-third of those who receiving federal financial aid. Some colleges audit every applicant of financial aid. False statements on the FAFSA may result in a penalty of $20,000 and/or prison time.

The Work-Study Program

If you are eligible, the Work-Study Program can provide a valuable opportunity in an area of your interest. This experience can help get you started in your career ahead of other graduates who don't have practical expertise in their field of study. Alternatively, a Work-Study position may be a paid quiet time to get studying done. This federally funded program pays 75% of a student's wage for mostly on-campus jobs for eligible students. This support gives an opportunity for the student to have a job where the employer pays little and where the student can gain valuable experience in a field where the employer otherwise would not have funds to hire them. If you are eligible, there are great ways to utilize this benefit, and some poor ones.

The best way to take advantage of this opportunity is to get work experience in scientific research or in an area that provides the student with hands-on experience that develops technical skills. For example, science or engineering students might find work that provides training and experience in a technical area.

- For careers in academia: working in the grants office can teach research methods and grant applications preparation.
- For careers in technology: working in the Office of Technology Transfer (in large universities) you may learn to do patent searches and understand patents.
- For science careers: working in a lab provides research experience such as growing cell lines, learning laboratory skills and doing data analysis.
- In any field, getting publications from your work will be a bonus.
- For students into music, theater, or film, look for opportunities in production and stagecraft.
- For everyone, leadership, event planning and coordination, or other managerial experience can be helpful.

Try to find a Work-Study position that will further your career. This will help you land a better job when you get out of school, putting you ahead of other recent graduates, especially if you are in a competitive field. Work experience with specialized equipment in technical fields, such as science, is hard to come by outside of the university. Getting authorship on publications may help further your career.

Another way to use the Work-Study opportunity is to find a job that has almost no demands. One, allowing you time to study or read assigned materials while being paid. Especially for your first year of college, a no-stress, paid, study-period can be a blessing.

I recently met a young woman paid to sit at the entrance to an on-campus museum that might see a couple of visitors during her shift. The rest of her time, she was at a comfortable desk in a quiet setting where she could study.

Look for a position that builds leadership abilities and useful experience. Try to avoid Work-Study jobs that have you working in the cafeteria, as a latte boy, doing secretarial, menial, or low skilled tasks. Those jobs will earn you a few bucks but are unlikely to provide a competitive edge when you graduate. They too are less likely to be enjoyable. Let the staff at the office that handles the Work-Study program know what type of position you are seeking, whether it is babysitting a rarely visited campus museum, or one working in the lab of a Nobel Laureate, which helps prepare your for a career. Consider working in different areas different years to get a wider range of experience in areas of your interest.

Honesty and integrity are absolutely essential for success in life - all areas of life. The really good news is that anyone can develop both honesty and integrity.

~Zig Ziglar

CHAPTER 19: SUMMATION

The future belongs to those who believe in the beauty of their dreams.
~Eleanor Roosevelt

The most salient feature in selecting a college or university is that it is appropriate for you, and you are likely to be happy and successful there. Chances for happiness are highest in a place where you have a social life that supports your success, and one you can afford. Try to select among colleges you feel will help you grow and develop as a person. Once you have your degree, it usually does not matter that much where you got it. The important thing for careers is that you get the education, diploma and credentials that your employer will expect.

Choosing a college is like a marriage. An individual might be able to make almost any marriage work. However, if your mate has different values and different goals than you do, wants to go in a different direction than you do, and spends limited shared resources on things you disagree with, the relationship will be a drag, and assuredly, you will both be unhappy.

Students are likely to be happiest in a school where other students move in the same direction they do. A Christian fundamentalist college might not be a great choice for an atheist. If you are exceptionally bright and dedicated, a community college is likely to be a snooze for you, and not help you develop your capacity.

A highly gifted individual should not have difficulty getting admitted to a great college. However, it does not take a high IQ to keep your bedroom neat and organized. In the same way, keeping your school work neat and organized, doing the ground work and learning to take the ACT, appropriately selecting classes in which you can excel, and being polite and on time make a huge difference in your test scores, grades and letters of recommendation. With planning, diligence, discipline, and maturity, it does not require genius to gain acceptance and thrive in an elite college.

Achieving a high ACT score is more preparation and planning than the forgone result of high intelligence. Many high IQ students are disappointed by their college placement test scores. While a high IQ certainly helps, maturity and focus are just as, if not more, important. These tests may reward students with the highest IQ's, but also reward students with good IQ's that are mature, organized, and reliable. These same traits make students successful in college.

The greatest advantage of earning a high GPA, scoring high on the ACT or SAT and spending time to write a great admission essay is not that it gets you into a prestigious school, but rather that it can provide you an affordable, quality education in a happy place. Insufficient funding for the high cost of college adds stress to the life of students and their families and is a common reason that students fail to graduate. With great scores, you may be able to attend a state school free or attend an exclusive private college for less than the price of attending a state college.

You may not be gifted; however, you can train yourself to be organized and responsible. You can learn the rules of grammar. You can train your brain to spot errors and learn the math required for the ACT test. If you are a not natural, it just takes more time and perseverance. You can learn to think analytically. Even if you are very bright, there are likely holes in your education or weak spots in your abilities. You may be a math wizard, but consider grammar trivial and of little value. It is easy to discount the things you're not good at or don't enjoy.

It is far better to master these areas than allow them to impede your progress. The sooner you plug those holes, the less they will trip you up and impede your success. The further you go in life, the more useful those basic, boring skills will be. It is worth the effort to tweak your academic performance. Especially, if you only have average intellectual gifts, your success will depend on honing your skills and optimizing organization and planning.

Perhaps you are not accepted, or offered a scholarship that allows you to attend an elite college. Perhaps the state college is your dream school. Maybe academic, financial, or family reasons limit your options, and it's your only real choice. You can get a great education at most state or community colleges. It will still take work; perhaps more work to succeed in these environments. Committed, mature students can get educated anywhere. See if you may be eligible for a school's honor program, which will provide an elite school experience, at a public university.

If you attend a university similar to the US Naval Academy at Annapolis, where virtually everyone graduates; do your work, and you will get through. Senator John McCain, a presidential candidate in 2008, graduated 894th out of 899 students, but he still graduated from one of the top ranked colleges. However, if you attend a college where less than half the starting students graduate within 6 years, assume that you need to maintain a grade point average in the top quarter of your class to ensure success.

At a less selective college, you may not be immersed in a community of highly intelligent, efficient, motivated peers. Nevertheless, strive to surround yourself with a circle of bright, engaged friends who are slated for success, and who rank in the top quarter of the class. In a less selective college, it may be easier to shine; to find opportunities to work with professors, to get hands-on experience or do research, and to earn high grades. In this way, these schools may provide greater opportunities to progress and attend the graduate university of your choice.

If your ship doesn't come in, swim out to it.

~Jonathan Winters

CHAPTER 20: SURVIVING COLLEGE

The best helping hand that you will ever receive is the one at the end of your own arm.

~Fred Dehner

Sustainable Fun

You can have fun, and party responsibly. This means you don't act in a way that jeopardizes your ability to have fun in the future. College life should be enjoyable, but this does not mean that you should dance blindfolded on the edge of a precipice.

Being kicked out of school, failing tests, taking risks that endanger your spine[*], being arrested, or unexpectedly becoming a parent can get in the way of sustainable fun. Take your cue on how hard to work and study, and how much partying is appropriate, from successful students at your school. If only half of the starting students in your program graduate and you perform like those in the lower half of the class, assume that you will not graduate either. Try to stay at least in the middle of the pack of those destined to graduate from your program. If you're in a major with a 20% graduation rate, you should aim to stay in the top 10% to of students.

Eluding Self Destruction

Chapter 11 listed some of the common reasons students fail or drop out.

- Academic Failure
- Drugs and Alcohol
- Pregnancy
- Economic Collapse

---

[*] Diving injuries are the most common spine injury. Never dive into waves, and always check to make sure water is deep enough before diving into it. River bottoms can change overnight.

Academic Failure: Perhaps you were not academically prepared. You arrive for your first semester and find that you do not have the background for your classes. At that moment, you are likely to conclude that you are a failure and want to hide from your friends and avoid speaking with your parents. You may feel isolated; however, I guarantee that you are not alone. Many high schools fail to prepare their students for college. Many students, perhaps most students, have academic difficulty while adjusting to their first semester of college.

First, have some faith in yourself. If you got into college, you are probably bright enough to get through. What you may be lacking is college 'street smarts'. Most first semester students are in a brand new environment and it takes some time to learn how to live away from home, balance social life and classes, and develop the study habits required to perform at college level.

CAUTION: Don't always follow the leader. That other freshman kid, the one with super confidence that seems to know all the ins and outs of the college, probably doesn't, and may be more lost than you. Look for a mentor; find someone that has experience and wisdom from surviving at the school for a couple of years.

Most students have a hard time in their first semester. You may feel that you are drowning in class work, and have to work harder than you have before. Some professors, rather than helping you, take pride in weeding out "weak students," and will suggest that you change major – do something less challenging. You may see friends and classmates drop calculus and abandon their engineering degree for one in dance therapy.

Don't do what I did. I wanted to study medicine, and asked my clueless college counselor what classes to take. He didn't know, so he loaded me up with the toughest biochem and physical chemistry courses on campus. When I walked into the classroom, most of my classmates knew each other; they had taken three or four semesters of chemistry together, but it was my first class.

I did not build a foundation; I struggled, got C's, and abandoned my dream; I thought I wasn't smart enough for medicine, got a worthless degree in psychology, and ended working in agriculture and construction as a laborer. It was a few years later, in the Peace Corps that a doctor friend asked why, since I was interested in health and medicine, I had not gone to medical school. He convinced me I could succeed. Even though I had bombed those college classes, it was not a lack of intelligence, but of foundation and preparation. After Peace Corps, I enrolled in medical school and graduated top of my class.

Chapter 1 advised finding the safe and sure path up the mountain. Especially during the first semester of college, make sure you plan and gather intelligence to find the best routes to success, and avoid risks of failure or trauma. Remember that many mountains with vertical cliffs, which are nearly impossible to surmount, have more accessible paths to their summit. These trails are usually going to be longer and still may be steep; however, they are much surer, safer, and more reliable ways of completing the trek to the top.

- Just adjusting to college life can be consuming. You need to complete prerequisites, but I suggest avoiding excessively challenging workloads the first semester. Especially if you have a scholarship that demands you maintain a certain grade point average, you may want to ease through your first semester of college with a light class load. If you can, take an easy elective and do a physical education class if you can for fun, fitness, and stress reduction.
- If you can, avoid taking the toughest classes the first semester of college. Calculus is a common obstacle for students. Unless you are a math ace, delay the most rigorous classes and areas where you feel weakest until you settle in. Take classes to build your abilities, not to highlight your weaknesses.
- Prepare: If there is a choice, research to find out which teachers are best, and most likely to help you move forward. You want professors that are great teachers, who make the

complex simple, and who help students learn. You want to avoid those who gleefully thin the herd, at least until you are confident that you will not be among those being culled. Find out from students a year ahead of you who are the best professors.

What makes a great class? The teacher makes the class interesting, makes complex concepts understandable, and doesn't burden students with busy work. The student learns a lot and gets a great grade.

Professor rating websites rate teachers on helpfulness, clarity, and easiness. Easiness can be a quality in your first semester, but after that, look for the best learning opportunities, not ones where you work and learn the least. Talk to students a year ahead of you about professors and try taking classes taught by the best teachers.

Even if you have no choice as to which professor you have, try to find out from previous students what the professor expects. Find out which materials they base tests on (homework, textbook, lectures, etc.). This can help you prepare better, and get better grades.

Online rating sites, such as www.ratemyprofessors.com, tend to be biased; easy teachers score well, and more demanding teachers are rated low, rather than assessing how much students learn in the class. Additionally, these sites are often several years out of date. Use these websites with caution. It is better to ask good students who have taken the classes at the school (perhaps through social media sites such as Facebook) what they have experienced.

- Follow your dreams. If it was easy, everyone would be successful. STEM degrees are more difficult than those in social work. Unless you change you mind about what you want to do, don't give up on you goals the first time you stumble. If you are going after a great career, expect it to be a challenge. Don't expect college to be as easy as high school. Expect some setbacks, and expect to work hard to overcome them. Expect to work harder than you have ever worked before. That is how you grow, get stronger, and move forward.

- Don't be afraid to ask for help. You may have been top in your class and never needed help before. Swallow any false pride, get help, and move forward.
- Act sooner than later. Especially in STEM classes, where knowledge and understanding are built vertically upon what you already know, any holes and weaknesses can cause catastrophic collapse and failure as you try to move forward. If you find you have deficits in some areas of your education, try to fill them. If you do not, your progress will be based on an unstable foundation, and you will fall further and further behind until you fail.

If you find you do not understand the material in class, get help immediately. The longer you wait, the further behind you will be and the more difficult it will be to climb out of the knowledge pit. If this happens, visit your professor or the counselor's office and get help. You may need tutoring, a change in classes, or perhaps just some reassurance. Most colleges are prepared to help and see this problem numerous times every year. Most colleges are obliging and understand it is part of their job to help you succeed. But you need to be willing to ask for help, and to do it as soon as you suspect there is a problem. Don't wait until it is too late; when your grades are failing, and your scholarship is in peril. In class, if something doesn't make sense, look around and see if everyone looks lost. If that is the case, ask the teacher to clarify.

Wikipedia and YouTube can be great educational resources to help understand vocabulary and concepts that you may have missed. You may be surprised by the educational material on YouTube that can help explain tough concepts. Often, when students are struggling in class, it is because they have missed one or two essential concepts or lack certain vocabulary that allows them understand the rest of the material. Sometimes, it takes very little to set things right if done soon enough.

While curiosity, conscientiousness, resilience, confidence, intelligence and emotional intelligence are all requisites, so is patience. Don't attempt to rush through learning. Students that try to rush through college and graduate school often end up losing their curiosity. It is not IQ, but rather independent, creative thinking, and persistence that differentiate successful graduate students from those who do not make it through.

Striving to quickly complete academic tasks can make learning and schoolwork a chore rather than a pleasure. It can kill creativity and curiosity. Avoid overloading or overworking yourself. It is counterproductive in the end. Leave time and energy for intellectual exploration and play.

Health

Another common contributor to failure is lack of sleep. If just about now you would like to reach out and tell me that I sound like your mother, then thank you for the compliment. During college, your body will still have a physiologic imperative for about 8.5 hours of sleep per night. It is easy to get involved with activities, friends, parties, dalliance, and even studying, and end with insufficient sleep for your brain to work at its best. Adequate sleep is a requirement for normal brain function. Study when you are awake and fresh, not when you are fatigued.

Nutrition is also essential. The brain cannot use high fructose corn syrup as fuel (fructose does not cross the blood-brain barrier; however, excess fructose is metabolized into fat in the liver). Eat real food and get sufficient sleep if you want to develop new neural synapses in your brain.

You may have heard of the freshman 15. It is actually only 1.5 (kg). This 3.5 to 4 pound average weight gain often occurs in the first couple of months of the freshman year. Fast food, fried food, fructose-filled soda pop, "free food" (unlimited food on a meal ticket), and friends (hanging out with social eating) can increase consumption. Lack of sleep also increases appetite. To prevent weight gain, don't count calories; rather eat healthy foods and avoid junk food.

If possible, enroll in a physical education or athletics class the first semester of college. Hopefully, this will provide a low-stress class, which fulfills a general education requirement, which is an opportunity to get you familiar with the athletic facilities available on campus. Look for an athletic outlet that you can enjoy throughout college and beyond. This may be a place to reduce stress and keep your brain working at a high level, plus, be a venue to diversify friendships, outside of your major.

Academic failure is more often a lack of maturity (organization, responsibility, and self-discipline) than lack of intelligence or knowledge base. Yes, it may be hard, but it is a lot harder if your brain is not functioning at full speed because of lack of sleep, lack of nutrition, or excessive stimulants, drugs or alcohol.

Class Work

Show up (on time) to class. Staying awake through the class and getting homework done are essentials, and for many classes, is nearly sufficient for earning a passing grade. Especially if you are not finding the academic work a breeze, get to class a few minutes early so that you can get a seat up front where it is easier to concentrate and hear the professor. Keep a calendar to make sure you organize your time and get assignments submitted when due. In college, the professors do not always repeat deadlines, so it is easy to forget when your term paper is due and when tests may be given.

Don't cheat to get ahead. It is likely to come back to haunt you. Would you want a doctor that cheated on their medical school exams to be operating on you? How about an airline pilot that cheated on the exams for in-flight emergency procedures? Don't plagiarize. It is easy for teachers to put any line from work you turn in into Google or Turnitin.com and find the original source.

After students get to college, ACT and SAT scores end up not being very good predictors of college success. A more reliable predictor is whether students show up for class. Maturity and responsibility trump native intelligence.

Don't let anyone push, cajole, harass, or embarrass you into doing things you don't feel are right for you, or you feel are unethical, dangerous, or imprudent. Be the best version of you that you can be. If someone pressures to compromise your values, tell your acquaintance that you have higher expectations of yourself and of them. If you are not comfortable doing this, leave the situation. A friend will support your efforts to improve yourself. Acquaintances that pressure you to compromise yourself and your values are not friends, and are likely trying to use you for their own benefit. If you have roommates that prevent your study, or compel you to do things you think are dangerous or wrong, it's time to change roommates. It is your life; you are an adult, you are responsible for the decisions you make. If you give up power over those decisions, you are giving up you rights and giving up on being an adult.

Be who you are and say what you feel, because those who mind don't matter and those who matter don't mind.

~Dr. Seuss

Drugs and Alcohol

Drugs and alcohol can easily be your ruin although it may take a few years to pickle your liver. Drugs, alcohol, and tobacco neither help you succeed nor help resolve problems. They will not solve calculus, chemistry, social, financial, nor emotional problems. It is impossible to show to how well you can hold your liquor. You only show how stupid you are. Use of stimulants, such as ADHD medications, for those without this condition, may give the illusion performance enhancement when studying for finals, but it does not work. While these drugs increase wakefulness and increase certain cognitive tasks, they increase attention to distractions and fail to increase academic performance[7]. If you do not have ADHD, these stimulants present real risks without net benefit.

Sex and Pregnancy

If you plan to have sex, use protection. Spontaneous sex may seem romantic at the moment if you are a newb, but usually seems stupid after the fact. If you don't plan to have sex, don't have it. Sex involves the life of another person, and potentially a pregnancy and child. It is an adult behavior; so if you want to engage in sexual behavior, be an adult about it, and take responsibility for it, including the emotional toll, pregnancy, or disease that may occur. By being prepared, many unwanted risks associated with sexual activity can be mitigated.

Party sex with someone you have known for a few hours is usually regretted. (I worked in a sexually transmitted disease clinic; most of the young bucks who thought they were getting lucky were getting something else!) Even if cultural and moral taboos are dismissed, sexual promiscuity is unlikely to provide sustainable happiness. Casual liaisons rarely lead to closeness or supportive friendships. Learning to build lasting bonds will serve you better. Intimacy does not require intercourse, and copulation in no way guarantees intimacy.

If someone wants to have sex with you within a day of meeting you, it is likely that, if the opportunity presented, they have had sex with a stranger the previous week, and they will have sex with different person next week. Doesn't make you feel special, does it? It does, however, put you at risk of whatever diseases that nice person might have been exposed to by the other nice people they had sex with and from the nice people those people had exposure to before that. When sex is part of an established relationship, it allows for planning and avoidance of risks. Men having sex with men have the highest risk for HIV.

If you don't want to have sex, it is your choice, not anyone else's. If the sex is not consensual, it is rape. If the other person is not fully sober at the time they consent, it is rape. If you want to have sex with someone, ask if they want to make love with you. Don't assume that you know what another person really wants, or what is best for them; that sort of thinking is for psychopaths.

About five percent of college women are raped every school year. Seventy percent of rapes involve alcohol; in most cases, the victim was drinking. In most cases, the victim knows the rapist, and the crime occurs in the home of the victim or rapist. Protect yourself by staying sober and being with sober friends. It may be a complex and difficult decision; however, if you are raped, and you don't report it, you are allowing other people to be raped. Nearly ten percent of non-prison rapes in the U.S. are of men.

Money and Economic Calamity

College may be accompanied by new financial freedom and responsibility. You may be getting college loans, grants, scholarship funds, and checks from your parents if you are lucky or have an educational IRA to draw upon. Agents on the college campus may be enticing you with your own credit card. This may be the first time you have a wad of cash you can spend. Trust me here; burning through money is easy.

You will have friends with economic disparities from you. If your friends are wealthier or less self-controlled with their funds, you may feel that you need to keep up with them in spending on eats, drinks, cappuccinos, buying clothes, attending concerts, and other nonessential niceties. If your friends have limited cash, it is easy to be generous and pay for the pizza and beer. However, you have your own economics, and need to live within those bounds.

Avoid luxury habits. Sodas, cookies, and beer should be treats, not just to survive financially, but also for your health. A daily double latte cappuccino at $7 is a $2000 annual habit. Smoking, soda pop, snacks and beer, and pay-per-view are not expensive items, but quickly add up. If you love smoothies, get a blender; make your own a quarter of the cost.

You need to budget the money you have and the money that you are borrowing. Set up a budget that is sustainable. Calculate how much you need to get through your degree, and how much you can spend per year, and per week. Put aside ten percent for emergencies, as they will arise. Even when you have a budget, try to conserve part of your weekly budget so that you can splurge for special events such as concerts, a new toy, or beach trips. You might get an opportunity to go to Europe, and money spent on lattes may be the difference between spending the summer in Biarritz and Rome and working as a fry cook at McDonald's.

Borrowing Money: Usually, college loans from the federal government are a good deal. The interest rate is usually lower than inflation, so you end up paying back dollars worth less than those you borrow by the time you are making payments. In addition, when you graduate you should have a higher income, so you should need to spend fewer hours working to make the same amount of money as you would now. Nonetheless, keep this borrowing as low as you can. Many young people are strapped with college loan payments that limit what they can do in their lives, especially young professionals that borrow to pay for both an undergraduate and a professional degree.

Don't lend money to, or borrow money from friends you want to keep. Don't borrow money from mafia loan sharks, who will crush your knees if you are late on payments. Treat other moneylenders, such as banks and credit cards, with the same aversion and trepidation you have for the mafia.

If possible, ask if your parent will cosign a credit card with a $300 to $500 limit. The $300 to $500 limit will be a safety net for both of you. This limit will *help* keep you from being tempted or able to overspend on the card.

A credit card allows you to save by buying books and other items on-line. It will allow you more freedom, and to respond to emergencies, such as, if your car breaks down, or you get stranded. However, don't use the card to borrow money or spend money you don't have. Be sure to pay off the balance on time every month. If you are late twice, most cards will increase your interest rate to the legal maximum. Moreover, that rate will stay high forever. Banks love college students. Students are typically financially naïve, disorganized and often miss timely payments. This makes them liable for high-interest rates and late fees, which are the main source of income from the cards. Recent legislation has curtailed some abusive banking practices, but high-interest rates and fees for missed payments still exist.

If you are new to adult life, it can be a surprise how much it costs to live a comfortable but un-extravagant lifestyle. Work out a budget and stick to it. If you are crossing the desert on foot and it's a 20-day journey, you don't want to run out of water on day 12. You want to have enough water in case the journey takes 30 days. Budget for the long haul.

Tuition and Fees: Don't forget there are many fees in addition to tuition. Lab classes, music classes, and other classes often have fees in addition to the tuition cost. Most colleges tack on "student body" fees. Make sure you account for these in your budget.

Living Costs: These are the recurring and unavoidable costs you will have. Most reoccur every month, but others, such as books, computer and other equipment, occur less frequently. Calculate your expected fixed cost per month. Divide the other costs, such as books and computer, over the semester or expected lifetime of the books or equipment.

Emergencies and Unforeseen Costs: I advise leaving a 10% set-aside of your discretionary money for the unexpected, for emergencies, and for your graduation move. Emergencies happen, and not surprisingly, usually without much warning. Having a reserve of cash can help you get through and recover from emergencies. What if your computer dies or takes a walkabout? Your car may need repair; you may need money for an emergency trip home. If you get sick or injured, even with health insurance, there may be co-pays for the doctor or emergency department visits, or costs for the medication. Health insurance will not pay for over-the-counter medications, such as antihistamines. You may not have dental insurance.

Living costs:

$_____ Clothing (purchases, laundry, detergent)
$_____ Room and Board or rent and food
$_____ Utilities (electricity, gas, water, sewer, garbage)
$_____ Transportation (to school if living off campus, car payments, gas and maintenance, trips home)
$_____ Communication (cell phone, phone, internet access)
$_____ Personal hygiene (haircuts, razors, deodorant, shampoo, dental floss, tampons, etc.)
$_____ Insurance (health, car, motorcycle)
$_____ Health (medication, dentist, copayments)
$_____ Debt payments (car, furniture, other loans)
$_____ Income taxes
$_____ School supplies (books, equipment, computer, pens notebooks, and other supplies)
$_____ TOTAL

Variable Costs and Voluntary Spending: In addition to the fixed cost, there are variable costs, many of which are not necessities. These costs are very important to include in your budget as they can deplete your budget.

Variable Costs:

$_____ Eating out and snacks, coffee, beer, dating
$_____ Cell phone/texting (going over your limit)
$_____ TV and online access (pay-per-view)
$_____ Entertainment (movies, concerts, parties, events,
                games, music, etc.)
$_____ Memberships, donations (gym, club, professional
                societies, church, etc.)
$_____ Personal extras (cosmetics, sports equipment, toys,
                musical equipment, guitar strings etc.)
$_____ Other (travel, gifts, vacations, etc.)
$_____ TOTAL

You will also need money upon graduation to move on: professional clothing for interviewing for a job, rent for housing or money to move and get started in a new town or in a graduate program in another state. Most apartments require first and last month rent plus a deposit to move in. Unless you have friends in the new city, it is hard to get started without a few thousand dollars handy for startup costs.

Sometimes an opportunity arises that is too good to pass up, and having set aside some cash allows you to take advantage of the prospect that would otherwise be missed. What if your best friend's roommate offers to sell his Stradivarius at less than a 10th of its street cost, and it would allow you to move up from the second-hand clunker you have been struggling with? What if your buddy just invented the best app you have ever seen, and needs a few hundred dollars in seed money from a partner to get it going?

Having even a small reserve can make the difference between being forced into financial conservatism with parsimonious frugality, and the ability to take some entrepreneurial risks. There is an important difference in the mindset of the wealthy and the middle-class wage slaves. The wealthy have the luxury to take risks with disposable assets available to them to create more wealth, while the middle class and the poor struggle to survive on the limited resources available to them. If you don't have any disposable savings, how can you take advantage of opportunities that involve financial risk?

Educational IRA funds may only be used for "qualified" educational expenses. These can include tuition, fees, books and supplies, room and board paid directly to the college or an amount limited to that the college allows for room and board. Taxes must be paid for non-qualified distributions taken from the Coverdell educational IRA. Somce most colleges do not require students to have a computer, this is not a qualified expense.

The rules are less strict for high schools, where educational IRA funds may be used to pay for a computer or other educational expenses, such as a muscial instrument needed to practice and play in a performing arts high school. If you have an educational IRA, the month before you graduate is a fine time to buy a computer to use in college, so that it will be a qualified expense.

Entrepreneurship

Do you even need a degree? Bill Gates, the founder of Microsoft, and Mark Zuckerberg, the founder of Facebook, are both college dropouts; both dropped out of Harvard. They were not sloths, but rather highly intelligent, exceedingly motivated entrepreneurs (risk takers) that saw opportunities that they refused to wait on. If Zuckerberg had not been in college, he probably would not have created the creepy, girl-rating site for his friends, which evolved into Facebook.

Remember when I joked about Harvard and egos in Chapter 11? Both Gates and Zuckerberg possessed unbounded self-confidence and extraordinary chutzpah, which empowered them to take risks.

Nevertheless, even as an entrepreneur, you need investors. In recent years, many colleges have started programs in entrepreneurship. It does not take a college degree to start a business, invent a new device, be a musician, professional athlete, or actor. However, most attempts in these fields do not have big payoffs. Most aspiring actors, musicians, artists, authors, and athletes cannot make a living at their chosen vocation. Most businesses fail within the first two years. Only a small percentage of patented inventions ever make money for their inventor. (I remain optimistic).

Pursue your dreams! However, you will likely need to support yourself while you work towards them. A back-up plan that provides alternative opportunities of success may be preferable to waiting tables when you're 40.

One of the greatest things about college is the social and intellectual interaction that occurs there. Online courses do not provide that. The pooling of various people together with their diversity of ideas broadens your intellectual perspectives and engenders new ideas. A good college exposes you to great minds, to students with different cultures and ideas, and to professors and students that force you to stretch your psyche. Weak students expect teachers to ladle out content as if they were holding a bowl in a soup line. For great students, however, it is more akin to playing a tennis match with a master who coaches you and challenges you to exceed them.

Money is a wonderful servant, but a stingy, cruel, abusive master.

The shortcut to success is avoiding shortcuts.

~Charly Lewis

If you take risks, you may fail. But if you do not take risks, you will surely fail.

~Roberto C. Goizueta

CHAPTER 21: INTELLIGENCES

"If you are in the investment business and have an IQ of 150, sell 30 points to someone else. What you need instead is an emotional stability and inner peace about your decisions."

~Warren Buffet

I'm a lot smarter now that I'm not as smart as I used to be.

~Charly Lewis

We often assume that individuals who create advances in technology and science, design great architecture, or find ways to cure diseases are rare individuals gifted with an unusually high IQ. This is a myth. *You don't need to be a genius to be a genius.* A central goal in writing this book it is to dissuade you from the mindset that it takes a high IQ to be successful, and to dispel any notion that a person can rest upon their intellect to carry them to success. An exceptional IQ is not a requirement for exceptional successful in life, and if you are gifted with a high IQ, it is no more than a single leg of a table; it will not stand on its own.

The IQ test is an assessment of an individual's facility in the use of information. IQ tests are designed so that they have an average score of 100 and a standard deviation (usually) of 15. This means that the test scores 68 percent of the population to have an IQ between 85 and 115 and about 16% have an IQ over 115. These tests (wrongly) assume the population of IQs is distributed in a normal (bell-shaped) distribution.

There is not a single IQ test, but rather several "brands," including the Wechsler, Woodcock-Johnson, Stanford-Binet, and the Kaufman Assessment. If more than one of these tests are administered to a single individual, it is not uncommon to find a 20-point difference in IQ test results. Different tests assess different aspects of analytic and informational intelligences.

IQ tests work well to evaluate certain abilities. These include reasoning, ability to form concepts and solve problems using new information, the ability to store and retrieve memory, reaction time, and processing speed. IQ also includes knowledge, ability to communicate, reading, writing, and computational skills, vocabulary, and visual and auditory processing.

These are important attributes and they correlate well to abilities that help to achieve academic attainment. Thus, a high IQ expedites test taking and earning an excellent GPA. The SAT is sometimes used to estimate IQ as it tests similar functions.

Having a decent IQ is pretty much a requirement for academic success. An IQ of 85 is the minimum required for entry into the U.S. military service. This is about the minimum IQ level required to successfully to graduate with a high school diploma.

It is difficult for individuals with an IQ of less than 100 to succeed and thrive in a four-year college, and rare for an individual with IQ below 90 to graduate with a bachelor's degree. Many individuals, however, in the 85 to 100 IQ range succeed and benefit from a two-year technical or trade program which may be earned in a community college.

The average college graduate has an IQ of about 112. The average IQ for medical doctors is reported to be about 125, with the great majority having an IQ over 120: the top 10 percent of the population. Elevated IQ indicates a facility with analytic processing and handling large amounts of information. Doctoral level degrees require abilities in these areas.

It is important to have a high enough IQ to do the work you want to do, but having excess IQ points does not provide much benefit. The most productive scientists, most successful musicians, businessmen, artists, journalists, and politicians are not the brightest ones in terms of IQ, but rather those who are the most creative and most productive. While a good IQ facilitates success in the non-academic (real) world, it is not a requirement.

The IQ Myth: IQ is confounded with genius as a result of work by Lewis Terman, an early twentieth-century researcher at Stanford. He popularized the definition of genius as an IQ of 140 or above. Since IQ appeared to be an innate trait, something that one was born with, by this definition, if not born a genius, an individual was simply out of luck. Additionally, the frequency of geniuses in the population could not be increased. IQ is a statistical score based on a theoretical distribution; only 38 out of ten thousand people are scored with an IQ of 140. If more high IQ individuals show up, the score shifts to limit the number of geniuses, according to Terman's paradigm. However, it is even worse. Terman got the math wrong; only about 13 out of ten thousand people rank the score of genius under his framework.

The word genius comes from the same word as genie, such as the spirit of Aladdin's lamp. The term genius is ascribed to people that influences others (for good or evil), through their distinctive character or spirit that embodies a quality. It refers to a person having a marked aptitude, skill, or intellectual prowess, manifested by creativity and productivity.

Success requires a range of abilities, which include IQ, but which also include maturity, persistence, perseverance, creativity, passion, self-confidence, and practical intelligence. Individuals in the top 5 percent of IQ rankings are no more successful in professional life than others in the top 25%. Genius is not a private reserve for those with rarefied IQs.

"Beauty is as beauty does," expresses the sentiment that beauty is much more than superficial appearance. A face that expresses warmth, humor, receptivity, and kindness instills a sense of beauty, while a cold, detached sneer is repelling even on a perfect face. Moving with grace and self-confidence is attractive, while an awkward and clumsy gait is not.

In the movie "Forrest Gump," Forrest says, *"Stupid is as stupid does."* Let me assure you that *genius is as genius does.* You don't need an IQ of 140. You don't need to be a genius to be a genius.

While a low IQ is very limiting in terms of professional access, the converse is not true. High IQ minds are notably democratic; they provide equal opportunity. High IQ individuals can be found in all walks of life and every profession, including doctors, lawyers, carpenters, janitors, cooks, bartenders, hotel house cleaners, and homeless beggars.

A high IQ not only does not predict success or happiness, it can act as a liability that impedes success. Many high IQ individuals fail to achieve much in their lives. One reason is that it makes classroom learning easy. High IQ kids can rely on native intelligence and get great grades without much work. Someone who learnt successful laziness should not expect to accomplish much in life. Some gifted children that have not had to work, begin to fail when they reach a complexity of education that requires active learning. It is not rare to find high IQ individuals that became frustrated by this and then just tuned-out.

Here is what the American College Testing (ACT) program found when it looked to see if test scores predicted success:

"The adult accomplishments were found to be uncorrelated with academic talent, including test scores, high school grades, and college grades. However, the adult accomplishments were related to comparable high school non-academic (extra-curricular) accomplishments. This suggests that there are many kinds of talents related to later success which might be identified and nurtured by educational institutions."

Not only are test scores unrelated to adult accomplishments, the ACT organization, which derives its existence upon tests to differentiate levels of academic acumen, suggests that schools should emphasize non-academic elements as part of education.

Additionally, a review of 43 studies found that a high college GPA did not predict success in adult life. You need to make good enough grades to keep your scholarship, but a high GPA does not assure real world success[8]. A study of physicists and biologists found that academic proficiency (college grades) did not predict which scientists would make significant contributions to science, be most productive, or held in highest esteem for their work by other scientists[9].

The elite colleges and universities place undue emphasis on high placement scores and grades in the selection process in an attempt to select the most capable students. This creates a bias towards individuals with high verbal and analytical intelligence. There is nothing wrong with these skills; nonetheless, these only represent a limited set of skills, insufficient to provide success.

Why do schools rely on a form of intelligence that appears to have limited range of augmentation? Partly because knowledge and verbal and analytical skills are easy to assess. How do you measure creativity? How do you measure passion, compassion, and perseverance in the classroom and on an application? Additionally, the universities have long selected for this type of intelligence, and thus, the university is a product of its own selection process. The fact that universities look at extracurricular activities in selection criteria demonstrates that they are cognizant of the limitation of academic testing in predicting success.

In the 18th century, few people had books, and no one had a hand-held calculator. It was important to memorize and learn to calculate. To communicate across a distance, you had to write. There were few reference libraries. Then, schoolhouse learning and memorization made sense. An educated man was one who spoke well, knew classical literature, and who could cipher.

By the 19th century, little had changed, however, there were telephones by the end of the century, and books were more available. By the end of the 20th century, we had electronic calculators. We now have smart communication devices that access the internet, and most human knowledge is accessible on demand from almost anywhere at any time.

Memorization is far less reliable or essential in a world where information increases and changes so rapidly. Today, an expert is someone who specializes in a narrow area and tries to keep up with his or her field. Education needs to adapt to training all students for success, not just those with the highest verbal IQ. Schools should promote a range of intelligences to develop highly capable and successful individuals.

What matters for success today?

- IQ: Enough to perform the requisite tasks efficiently
- Grit: To persevere.
- Creativity and Vision: To make something new.
- Conviction: To perceive that benefits outweigh the risks.
- Skepticism: Things may not be as they appear.
- Intellectual honesty: Love the data you hate.

Intelligence: You need to be intelligent enough to learn and process content so that you can build knowledge and know-how, and move on to the next challenge in life. In school, this means getting good grades so that you can graduate and apply what you have learned.

Grit: Not grits, the hard corn, treated with lye and ground to make a Southern porridge, but rather persistence and tenacity[10]. Grit is a psychological trait that allows an individual to maintain interest and effort for the long haul. It is perseverance and passion for attaining long-term goals. If you hope to succeed, you need to stick with your goal, and not abandon it when things move slowly or run into difficulties. To succeed in something innovative or difficult, one must persevere despite inevitable failures and adversity. Gritty individuals maintain determination and motivation over long periods without short-term accolades or positive feedback.

Grit increases with age throughout life. Grit is independent of intelligence and is sometimes lacking in highly intelligent individuals who have not needed to develop it for success in school.

Success requires sufficient interest and passion in an area that a person dedicates time and energy into their projects and craft. One does not become fluent on a musical instrument in days. Most people can learn play an instrument in 20 hours. To become expert, it takes hundreds or thousands of hours. If you do not enjoy the activity, whether it is laboratory science or shredding tunes on the guitar, you would be a fool to dedicate several hours a day for several years to mastering a skill.

Creativity: Genius requires creativity. Some people succeed in life doing the same things over and over, but do little more than act as a machine. It takes creativity to do something innovative or outstanding. This is where we still outperform computers.

Rather than promoting creativity, education often acts to purge it. As we move to more performance-based academic assessment and tighter educational budgets, creativity is seen as a luxury with limited merit. The loss of creativity is not limited to the art and music programs, many of which have been curtailed. During most of schooling and almost all testing, there is a single correct answer. Anything else is penalized as wrong. Even in literature classes, bright students often figure out what the teacher expects, rather than explore what they perceive.

One aspect of creativity is finding multiple answers to a problem and then exploring and testing those solutions. Creativity involves looking at an issue, letting ideas percolate, and generating something new. It involves taking risks, as some of those ideas, probably most of those ideas, will not work out, or will not be advantageous over current methods. Nevertheless, the reward can be great when one does explore new ideas. Sadly, education and testing are designed to confine answers to a foregone singularity.

Lock-step, Bam-ba-bam!!!
Lock-step, Bam-ba-bam!!! Lock-step, Bam-ba-bam!!!
Lock-step, Bam-ba-bam!!! Lock-step, Bam-ba-bam!!! Lock-step, Bam-ba-bam!!!

"Of course our school budgets for creative activities! Just look at our music program!"

All children are born artists. The problem is to remain an artist as we grow up.

~Pablo Picasso

Conviction: Genius requires conviction. This is a sense of sureness that you will achieve your goal. Not only is your goal within reach of your abilities, but that the golden apple is already hanging there on the tree, with your name on it, waiting for you to complete the requisite steps so that you can step through the gates to pluck it and claim what is rightfully yours. This may be audacity; however, if you don't believe in yourself, you are unlikely to persevere in attaining your goal.

Skepticism: It takes a suspicious mind. Don't assume that the obvious answer is the correct one. Look for certitude.

There is a key difference that distinguishes M.I.T. students from those who attend lower performing colleges. For M.I.T.

students, the first impression on a trick question is the same as for most other students; however, they don't take the bait. They back check and test the answer, and then look for another solution when they find the first one was incorrect.

To succeed in creating something new, testing and questioning every aspect will allow breakthroughs and disprove dead-end answers that lead only to failure.

Intellectual Honesty: Testing and experimentation often provide results or data that do not fit the expected picture. Rather than ignoring, forcing, fudging, or faking data; try to understand what is says. It may be inconvenient to let the data be a teacher, however, this is what leads to breakthroughs. Get comfortable with uncertainty. Be open to let new data change your mind.

What Can be Done?
- IQ: It is not immutable
- Grit: It grows on you
- Creativity and Vision: Take a risk
- Conviction: Success breeds success
- Non-certitude: Trust, but verify
- Be honest even when it inconvenient

Raising IQ: Although many studies demonstrate that children with higher IQs continue to have to higher IQs as they mature, this does not mean that positive intervention to augment IQ is impossible.

We are muscle heads, and the areas we exercise get stronger. When a person loses their vision due to an accident, the brain is rewired to use sound and other senses to learn about the environment. Many blind people become sonic geniuses. Face readers learn to see micro-expressions that most of us cannot see. Musicians use their brains in ways I cannot. When children are out of school for long periods, their (academic) IQs fall. Their brains don't shut off; they just grow in different ways.

You can improve your IQ if it is something you are willing to work at, or (better) if something you enjoy doing correlates with IQ-type activities. You can raise your IQ by staying in school and getting an advanced education, especially if concentrating on analytical and problem-solving skills. Becoming fluent in a second language or in music increases IQ. Verbal abilities can be improved by reading aloud and focusing on clear articulation.

Good nutrition and sufficient sleep are essential for brain vitality and development, especially during the years when the brain is growing. A healthy brain learns better.

Once someone has reached an IQ of somewhere around 120, having additional IQ points doesn't seem to translate into any measurable real-world advantage.

~Malcolm Gladwell

Grit: Grit is learned, and increases throughout life; the average grit score is higher in individuals over 65 than those 55 to 65; scores at 55 to 65 years old are higher than for those who are 45 to 55. Grit is learned through experience. You can become grittier. It takes perseverance and trust that you can succeed. This is one reason why success breeds success. This is why, while you want to push the envelope to do more; you want to do things that you can succeed at, and avoid things that will defeat you.

To succeed at something innovative, something creative, you need to understand what failure is and what failure is not. Failure is a teacher, showing us something we did not know, helping us refocus our efforts. Failure is not defeat. Defeat occurs when you give up.

When it is dark enough, you can see the stars.

~Ralph Waldo Emerson

Failure is another steppingstone to greatness.

~Oprah Winfrey

I can accept failure, everyone fails at something. But I can't accept not trying.

~Michael Jordan

Creativity: Creativity entails risk. It requires experimentation; not all experiments go as planned. It requires a willingness to have failure as an outcome. When you have extra savings, you can take a bit of risk with those extra dollars if you are not worried about survival. When you have just barely enough to get by, you don't take risks. You stick with what you know – even if you don't like your situation. Better the devil you know. Better hungry than starved. To support creativity you either need some savings (or extra margin in your grade), or a boss (teacher) who understands creativity, and is willing to support you even when the creative process is not productive.

When you are confident in your own survival, and have leeway, you can risk some disposable assets. Failure can be tolerated without risking defeat, thus, the risk is manageable. When you have a margin of safety, you can experiment, be creative, and try new avenues. A creative environment rewards taking manageable risk while preventing defeat or painful outcomes. This latitude is required to experiment, to be creative, to hold out, and persevere.

Creativity requires the courage to let go of certainties.

~Erich Fromm

Creativity is the greatest expression of liberty.

~Bryant H. McGill

Creativity is allowing yourself to make mistakes. Art is knowing which ones to keep.

~Scott Adams

Conviction: Believe in yourself. During medical school, I think that every one of my classmates thought that we were already doctors, just waiting on the trifling detail of completing the degree before being handed our title. Looking back from the podium on graduation night, with a diploma in my hand, I realized that it had been a fallacious vision, and how much further I still had to go to be a physician. However, if I had not believed that the doctor was already in me, I doubt that I would have invested the years of study, risking the loss of other opportunities to achieve that goal.

A person who doubts himself is like a man who would enlist in the ranks of his enemies and bear arms against himself. He makes his failure certain by himself being the first person to be convinced of it.

~Ambrose Bierce

Non-certitude: Don't believe everything you believe. Get into the habit of proofing your assumptions. There will be traps on the ACT and SAT tests where they want to you to go for the obvious answer. Take a moment to make a reality check.

Make back testing your assumptions a habit. It is easy to be lazy, to select the first attractive answer, and then move on. Demand a higher level of confidence. Gut level decisions are lower level thinking, appropriate only when there is no higher-level data to rely on.

Intellectual Honesty: Make sure your data is good, and if not, find out why. Don't be painted into a corner by preconceived notions. Try to understand and differentiate between convictions and values, and beliefs. Individuals who think analytically and reflectively are more likely to question their precepts and change childhood views to accommodate their life experiences. They are more likely to question authority. Meanwhile, individuals who tend to be intuitive thinkers are more likely to hold on to conventional, conservative, and preconceived notions. It is O.K. not to know everything. It's far better to admit you just don't know, than to make decisions based on ideology, that are just as likely to be wrong as right.

The problem with any ideology is that it gives the answer before you look at the evidence, so you have to mold the evidence to get the answer you have already decided you have to have. It doesn't work.
~Bill Clinton

Other Intelligences

Practical Intelligence: Practical intelligence is the trait of being organized and thorough. Although it may seem incompatible with laziness, it is a lot less work to be organized and do things correctly the first time, than to cut corners or be sloppy and have to repeat your work.

You can train yourself to be organized, keep things orderly, and get things done on time. Using a calendar, organizing paperwork, doing the groundwork, and planning ahead increase the probability of success and lower the risk of failure. If you're going to have habits, they might as well be good ones.

Emotional Intelligence: Emotional Intelligence (E.I.) can also be learned. E.I. includes self-awareness, self-control, social skills, empathy, and motivation. The first step to improving your E.I. is being aware of what you are feeling. After you are aware of your own feelings, it becomes easier to be cognizant of how those around you are feeling.

Leadership: One of the college activities that best correlated with later real-world success was extracurricular activities that nurtured the individual toward developing leadership skills[11]. The other helpful activity was hands-on experience in scientific research; however, this type of experience is difficult to obtain outside of a university environment.

There are opportunities for leadership in clubs, charities, and other organizations, which help develop these skills while in college. However, once a person graduates, they most often find themselves on the very bottom of the totem pole in their workplace. If you want to succeed, leadership is an essential skill. It is tough to get a chance for leadership if you have to wait for your supervisors to retire or die before you can move up.

Use opportunities in college to get hands-on experience in scientific research if this is your area. Take leadership opportunities when they arise.

Opportunity: Many people think opportunity is a benefit that arrives out of the blue, but beware of strangers offering candy and free rides in windowless vans. Scammers exploit greed and sloth, and many people are enticed by frauds that look like an easy get-rich-quick, too good to be true bargain, or once in a lifetime opportunity.

Opportunity may knock only once, but temptation leans on the doorbell.

~Anonymous

Real opportunity, however, can be recognized by its close resemblance to work. The best opportunities are those that provide a matrix in which a person can transform themselves. Education and work experience may provide such opportunity. Nevertheless, transformation is not something that happens to you – but rather a side effect of your efforts.

Opportunity does not knock, it presents itself when you beat down the door.

~Kyle Chandler

Luck is what happens when preparation meets opportunity.

Lucius Annaeus Seneca

Steve dropped out after a few semesters; his parents hadn't put enough money aside for Reed, the private, liberal art college he attended. He spent the next few years living on a commune that had an apple orchard in Oregon, traveling to India to seek enlightenment, and meditating at a Zen meditation center.

He worked occasionally to get enough cash to get by, and would then return to the Zen center until his funds were depleted. He was in need of some cash and had an idea. It was 1975, and nerdy computer aficionados were learning to assemble small computers. Steve had a buddy, Woz, an electronics wiz. Steve's idea was to have Woz design a circuit board for the nerds, build 100 boards, sell them for $10 more than they cost, and split this $1000 profit between them. He walked, barefoot, into a computer electronics shop to try selling a sample circuit board. The proprietor was not interested, but instead proposed that Steve use the circuit boards to build fifty $500 computers, which would yield $5000 in profits. With this, Apple Computer was born.

In a free society, every opportunity comes with three obligations. First, you must seize it. You must mold it into a work that brings value to others. Second, you must live it. Opportunity is nurtured only by action. Third, you must defend the freedom to pursue opportunities. You must embrace these three obligations as if the future of the United States depended on it. In fact, it does.

Robert C. Goizueta

Opportunity dances with those who are already on the dance floor.

~H. Jackson Brown. Jr.

It's those who wait for their ship to come in who are always missing the boat.

~Anonymous

The intrinsic contract in any job, and perhaps in every relationship, is to contribute more value than you take. Even children are expected to bring more joy and fulfillment than grief into their parent's lives.

~Charly Lewis

CHAPTER 22: MORE THAN APPEARANCE

Beauty is what beauty does...

~Anonymous

Society is a shallow place. We make snap judgments about each other based on superficial information. Xenophobia and other prejudices emanate from subconscious, instinctive urges befitting coddled childish minds. There are all sorts of prejudices, and our success in life is often influenced by things that have nothing to do with our abilities, character, or quality of our work.

On a primal, instinctual level, we make several near instant judgments about people when we first see them.

Are they our tribe?
Are they hostile?
What is their gender?
Are they healthy?
Are they fertile?

First, we assess if they are a danger to us. Then we assess if they are potential mates. Pretty savage isn't it? Living in society, most of us have learned to override some of our natural biases; however, they largely remain until we get to know the person.

Two of these subconscious judgments, health, and fertility, correlate with physically attractiveness. In a primitive world (like ours,) hanging out with a diseased individual is risky. So, we avoid and are less comfortable being around individuals we perceive as being unhealthy. Another genetic imperative is selection of mates likely to provide healthy offspring. Our subconsciously determined visual assessment of physical attractiveness is largely an assessment of health and fertility. Smell is also used, especially by females, in mate selection.

We interpret health and vigor on several cues. They include unblemished skin; a symmetrical face and body; an elegant, even gait; and a relaxed mien; as these are all signs of health. Men who appear muscular and fit and women with a narrow waist give the appearance of fertility and thus fit the evolutionary precept of beauty.

Appearances affect how we are perceived. If I walk into a room to see a new patient and their clothes are disheveled and their hair straggly and unkempt; part of my job as a doctor will be to do a mental health and social assessment. I need to determine whether the person is able to take care of themselves; are they mentally ill, do they have resources to get their medications, do they live in a stable environment where they will be able to get and take medications properly. I usually skip these assessments on patients that come dressed and groomed as professionals.

Attractive individuals are assumed more intelligent, healthier and, more resilient. Physically attractiveness increases access to success in our society. Attractive people earn more and achieve better positions at work. You may notice that the more popular and well-liked students in your school are usually attractive.

This may seem unfair. Nevertheless, except for the truly unfortunate, being attractive depends much more on nurture than nature. We may be stuck with our genetics, and may never be strikingly beautiful or movie star handsome, but most of us can model our appearance to a level of physical attractiveness that serves us well, providing us access to success. It does take an investment of time and intent to enhance our attractiveness.

It is often worth the effort to fashion our appearances to fit the role we seek. Appearing clean and well groomed, having a dancer's posture, wearing clothes that fit well and an appropriate hairstyle and maintaining a calm countenance, all indicate health and make a person more attractive.

When I visited Stanford on the first day of their school year, I was struck by how healthy and attractive this set of young people were. When I watched a class of graduating high school seniors, those graduating summa cum laude stood out from most of their classmates as being especially attractive. But, these successful students were selected by GPA, not looks, and photos are not part of the selective college application process. The health and spirit of these young people were evident. It seemed obvious that they were loved by their families, had self-confidence and composure, and were eager to take on challenges.

Physical attractiveness is based on health, and so is academic ascendence. You can do this too. You can also fake it for a while with make-up and surgery, but you can't fake health for long.

The most important component to health and attractiveness is beauty sleep. In a Swedish study, researchers presented pictures to untrained observers of individuals who were either mildly sleep deprived or with sufficient sleep. These observers ranked the sleep deprived individuals as less attractive and less healthy[1]. The lead scientist concluded, "Sleep is the body's natural beauty treatment. It's probably more effective than any other treatment you could buy." As mentioned in previous chapters, sufficient sleep is required for learning and memory consolidation, and having fast reaction times.

Exercise not only makes us healthier, more attractive, and less overweight, it makes our brains work better. Like sleep, exercise and cardiovascular fitness correlate with test of working memory and executive function; the parts of the brain used in problem solving. You do not need to run marathons, but you do need exercise. The *minimum* exercise required for brain health is equivalent to walking 20 minutes per day; about one mile.

Clearly, diet is associated with health. Most Americans do not get enough green vegetables in their diet, and they eat excessive fatty, fried and preserved foods.

Avoid high fructose corn syrup; your brain cannot use fructose as fuel.

Acne: The foods best documented to cause acne are certain dairy products; those high in lactose. Skim milk is 2 – 4 times as likely to cause acne as compared with whole milk. Cottage and cream cheese also increase acne. Hard cheeses are not high in lactose and are not associated with risk for acne. Good health prevents acne: avoid junk food; get sufficient sleep and exercise. To lower risk of acne, shampoo at least 3 times a week, gently wash your face twice a day and change your pillowcase at least once a week. Medical treatment can prevent acne and scarring.

The two nutrients most commonly deficient in the American diet are magnesium, which is found in the center of every chlorophyll molecule in green leaves, and vitamin D_3, from sunshine during your 20-minute daily walk. If you live north of the south, however, you live too far north for the sun to make vitamin D in your skin during six months of the year. Washington DC and Indianapolis get too little sunshine for people to make vitamin D October to March. Even in the south, if you don't get out much, or have dark skin, you may benefit from a vitamin D_3 supplement.

Looking fit, healthy and attractive does not need to be expensive. Most people can make marked improvements in their appearance with a moderate effort. It does however takes attention. Many people, especially young people, are naturally beautiful. Nonetheless, most of those we perceive as beautiful put effort into their physical appearance.

If you have not grown up in a home or community that placed value on outward appearances, stylish clothing, make-up, hairstyling can seem to be nothing other than vanities. Certainly, considerable wealth may be spent on clothing and accessories, or plastic surgery.

A survey of 2800 human resource managers, the people who make hiring and promotion decisions, revealed that the top reasons qualified candidates didn't get the job were:

- Body piercings
- Bad breath
- Visible tattoos
- Wrinkly clothing, and
- Messy hair

1. Body Piercings: Other than a single piercing for earrings, avoid visible piercing jewelry for interviews. For men, if you don't think it will help with an interview, leave it off. This also applies for photographs, which might be seen on a Facebook page, or elsewhere you want to present yourself in a professional light.

2. Bad Breath: the most common cause of halitosis is a dirty tongue. Hold water in your mouth and brush your tongue when you brush your teeth. Waterpik or flossing may also help. When you are done, the tongue should be pink, not white or yellowish. Sinus and lung infections can also cause foul breath. If you eat garlic, it will stay in the breath for a day or so; avoid it before interviews. Don't smoke.

3. Although a tattoo may only cost $100, its real cost may be thousands of dollars, per year, in lost salary. Removing a tattoo can easily cost $10,000. Individuals with exposed tattoos are perceived to be less educated, less acquiescent, more intransigent and vagarious, thus more difficult to manage and work with.

If you want to express yourself with body art, do it with a radical hair cut, dyed fluorescent green, and clothing styles, or a henna drawing. When you tire of these, you can let your hair grow out, pick a new hair color, change your fashion, and wash the drawing off. Why would a person think they will still admire body art that he or she likes today, in 10 or 20 years, when it is blurring? Ask yourself, would you choose the same tattoo today that you thought was cool when you were nine?

4. Messy hair: see below.

5. Wrinkly Clothes: Iron your clothes for interviews and other occasions when you will be judged (everywhere). Use permanent press clothing to look sharp. Wear clothing that fits you well.

Since physical attractiveness is closely tied to success and improves self-esteem, efforts to improve appearance can be an astute investment into your future, rather than an indulgence in vanity.

I grew up with a distinctive schnoz. Indeed, my nose bore what my mother humorously acclaimed a "pronounced Romanesque grandeur." The nose is more than a hood ornament, and mine did not exchange air well. After a plastic surgeon I knew suggested it, I accepted his offer to alter it. If you don't have problems with yours, it is hard to appreciate what a luxury it is to breathe freely through your nose.

I had known that my model had not fit my face well; however, what was stunning was how differently people treated me after my face-off with the surgeon. Now that I looked more typical, people were friendlier and more open with me. I recall telling the same joke that had people looking at me askance, now had people laughing with me. Before, if I took initiative at work, I was accused of usurpation, perfidy, or sedition. Now, if I did the same, I received praise. It became easier to be hired for better jobs.

You may think this made me happy. In fact, it made me indignant. It miffed me that I had been often appraised upon my appearance. I felt that should be judged, instead, upon the content of my character.

I'm grateful for the benefits of the surgery; however, I remain troubled by how superficially people assess each other. I abhor racism and other forms of prejudice. If someone looks different, he or she may be assumed to be a weirdoes, dubious, perhaps a pernicious miscreant, when they are just unfortunate in their appearance. Some of us can rectify our nonconformity. I was fortunate. Not everyone can remedy his or her "deviance."

Orthodontic braces or other medical intervention may be appropriate for improving physical appearance. The pearly white smile is not only a sign of health and vitality; it is a sign of non-aggression, one of the primal, instinctual cues. Poor dentition gives the impression of a sick, effete individual.

Style

Some of us lack a sense of style, don't care, or perceive themselves as unattractive, and thus, don't make an effort. Most of us can use the eye of an expert in improving our appearance. Don't be shy about asking a friend with a sense of style, or asking a professional in the field, how you might improve your dress, hairstyle, and other components of your physical appearance.

When clothes don't fit correctly, it can look like something is wrong. A person who is overweight and wearing well fitting clothing may look big, but if they wear clothing that is too tight, it looks like they are rapidly gaining weight. If clothes are too loose, it looks like the person is losing weight, which on a primal level sends a subliminal message that they may have a wasting disease, perhaps infectious, and that should be avoided. Well-fitted clothing provides an air of competence, while poorly fitting clothing suggests use of cast-offs.

Look for clothes that fit you well. Dressier clothing especially, comes in many sizes and cuts; however, you may not find these in stock at most retail outlets. Most men's clothing dress clothing comes in a "classic cut" which looks stodgy and baggy on young men. Thin men might look for fitted, modern, slim, or athletic cut clothing. Young women may prefer modern, curvy, petite, or junior clothing styles to get the best fit for their body.

Find the size and cut which suits your body best, then look for them online, rather than trying to make do with what may be in stock at your local store. There will likely be better selection and prices online. If you order clothing from a store with a nearby retail outlet, there may be no shipping charges to pick them up and try them at the store. Change clothing size when your body changes so that you look your best.

Dress the part. People tend to assess each other at face value. If someone is wearing a police uniform, most people assume the person has some civil authority. If they dress in business garb, suit, and tie, they assume a different type of authority (e.g.; expertise or control of capital.) The way a person dresses, their costume, tells others their station in society. Choose the costume you wear according to the role you want to play. There are times you may want to be pegged as a rebellious youth down in the 'hood', and other times when you prefer to be identified as a fast-tracked upcoming executive. You will always get more respect when you are clean and well groomed, even as a rebel.

Posture

Poor posture is endemic in high school students. Although postural problems may require medical evaluation and treatment, the most common problem seen in adolescents is slouching, (nag, nag, nag.) This postural predicament results from spending too much time seated. When we spend much of our day seated, we learn to set our posture using our eyes rather than the inner ear, which we use for balance. If you have poor posture, trying to stand straight feels uncomfortable and unnatural. The muscles that should be used to stand can become imbalanced and weak. Additionally, walking while wearing a backpack that weighs over 10% of your body weight, will throw off your posture and balance, and train you to slump.

Looking from a profile, when standing, the opening of your ear canal should be directly above the mid-shoulder, the trochanter prominence of the hip, the center of the knee and over the ankle.

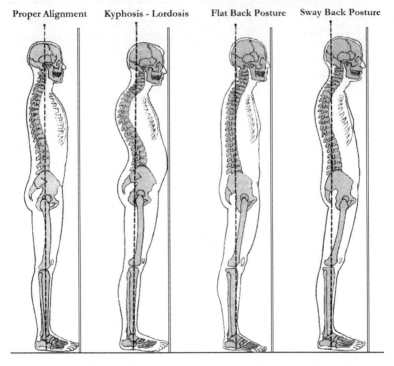

Proper Alignment   Kyphosis - Lordosis   Flat Back Posture   Sway Back Posture

Dancers have beautiful postures, in part because they depend on balance. Try this: stand with your eyes closed, and dance around (without running into things) for 15 seconds. With your eyes still closed, stop, and stand with your feet shoulder width apart, eyes straight forward, with 90 percent of your weight resting on your heels and 10% on the rest of your feet, for several seconds until you feel balanced; then open your eyes. This should give good posture. The nose should not touch the wall when standing with the toes facing the wall.

Hair

As adults age, aside from losing hair, hairs on the scalp become about 20 percent finer. This results in limp, flat looking hair. When hair has not been washed, it also appears limp and flat. Thus, clean, groomed hair provides the perception of youth and vitality. As mentioned above, messy hair is a common reason for not getting a job. Healthy mammals groom themselves and each other. The primal impression of someone with well-groomed hair is that they are healthy, loved, and cared for. The instinctual reaction to someone with messy hair is that the individual that has either been rejected by or lost its family, perhaps due to disease. Such individuals are subliminally considered a risk. Keep your hair clean and neat. If you have difficulty maintaining neat hair, consider a hairstyle that demands little care.

Hairstyles frame the face and change the perception of the person. A study by a professor of Women's Studies at Yale University found that hairstyles influenced observers' perceptions of the person within seconds.

Women with styled hair (any style) were perceived as sexier, but less intelligent. Women with very short hairstyles were seen as more confident and outgoing, but less sexy. Women with long blond hair were seen as more affluent, but more narrow-minded. Women with medium length casual styles were seen as good-natured and intelligent.

Longer hair is an indicator of health and provides an impression better health and youthfulness in women. Long hair make a stronger impact on the perception of health and attractiveness in less attractive women, but only slightly raises the attractiveness and perception of health in very attractive women[12].

Men with front flip back hair were perceived as confident and sexy, but self-absorbed. Men with longer hair were perceived to be less well off, but more open-minded. Men with hair parted to one side were perceived to be more intelligent, but narrow-minded.

Select a hairstyle that projects the image you want for yourself. The most important component of hair is that it appears well groomed: that the hair is clean, shiny, not dull, matted, or lifeless. On a primal, subliminal level, this will provide an image of health, vigor, and vitality. It suggests that you have people that care for you and that you are valued.

Get exercise so that not only do you look healthy, but you feel healthy and attractive.

People are like stained - glass windows. They sparkle and shine when the sun is out, but when the darkness sets in, their true beauty is revealed only if there is a light from within.

~Elisabeth Kubler-Ross

Of life's two chief prizes, beauty and truth, I found the first in a loving heart and the second in a laborer's hand.

~Khalil Gibran

The weirder you're going to behave, the more normal you should look. It works in reverse, too. When I see a kid with three or four rings in his nose, I know there is absolutely nothing extraordinary about that person.

~P.J. O'Rourke

If you can learn quickly from your own mistakes, you're ahead of the game. If you can learn quickly from others' mistakes, you've won the game.

~Anand Chokkavelu

APPENDIX A: MILESTONES

A pessimist sees the difficulty in every opportunity; an optimist sees the opportunity in every difficulty.

~Sir Winston Churchill

Planning is important for getting things done on time. Here is a brief outline for scheduling tasks in preparation for college.

Freshman Year: Sketch out the classes you plan to take during high school. Decide on a foreign language; many colleges require two years to three years of foreign language credits. Join clubs and extracurricular activities that you enjoy. Look for opportunities that provide a potential avenue for leadership.

Find out about summertime program activities that might be available to you throughout your high school years. Try to have at least one accomplishment that you can put on your CV every summer. This may be work experience, being a camp counselor or high adventure. You want to make sure that it does not appear that you slept in, played video games and watched T.V. for three months each year. Many college applications ask how you spent your summers.

Begin your CV. Add to it whenever you participate in extracurricular activities, volunteer, or win an honor or award. Record the hours you spend on these activities.

Sophomore Year: Start studying for the ACT test. Four practice tests are available at this book's supplemental material web page: https://sites.google.com/site/collegeprepguidebook/. Use the password "sunshine" (no quotation marks) if needed for this or other encrypted materials provided on this website.

The best time to take the SAT or ACT is probably mid-year during the 11th grade with enough time to repeat, it if need be, at the end of that year. ACT scores, on average, go up about 2 points per school year for average students and 3 points a year for top level students. Ten states now use the ACT, and others may begin using it or the new SAT, as a standard test of high school competency. This may mean that your state, rather than you chooses the test date. Make sure you have time to prepare well, as it can raise your scores as much as two years of school would.

Continue extracurricular activities that you enjoy and seek new opportunities for growth exploration and leadership. Prepare for and take the PSAT. Work on your writing skills. Look for academic competitions, which you are likely to enjoy, that can yield some awards or honors.

Junior Year: Take AP Language course if you have not already taken it. This should help you write better essays for your college applications, and do better on the reading sections of the placement tests. Prepare for the ACT and/or SAT and sign up to take them during you second semester of your junior year.

The deadlines for registering for these tests are about 5 weeks ahead of the test, so it is in December for the January SAT test. The ACT is offered twice, and the SAT three times during the spring. Both are also given in June. Register early, as seats may fill up at nearby test centers. If you think you may want a second go at the test, plan to do it in June. The fall tests results may come in late for early admission applications.

Register at two scholarship websites.

Research your college choices. Determine which are in line with your GPA and test scores, and select schools where you would be in the top 3/4^{ths} of the class. You can get an idea of the scores needed at CollegeProwler.com, in admission area for each school. Google the "Net Cost Calculator" for each school, to see if your family can afford it, or use the one on the College Board website to look at several schools.

Make sure you have taken required classes and SAT subject tests that might be required by some schools. You will need to prepare for them and take them during your junior year. Decide on your top choices, and select at least one back-up school you would be happy to attend and that you are confident will accept you. Try to visit the schools that you are interested in. A few schools give preference to students that have shown interest by contacting or visiting the school. See when they have open house or events for prospective students, and try to visit those you can.

Summer after Junior Year: Update your C.V. or start one if you have not. Print a copy of the Common Application and fill it out. Start working on ideas for your admission essays.

High-achieving students from middle or lower-income homes, (income less than $60,000/year) wishing to attending top-ranked private colleges, should check out the QuestBridge summer program at www.QuestBridge.org. Applications open in February. Students eligible for QuestBridge National College Match should start their applications early in August. The deadline is in late September. Applicants need to prepare their supplemental materials for each school early – deadlines are very tight, leaving only a few days after notification on October 22nd to get the applications submitted. The most prepared are the most likely to win.

Senior Year: By September 1, you should have created a list of colleges that you want to apply to. Read their applications web page, so that you know what they will be expecting, and know the application deadlines. Put them on your calendar.

Many colleges, especially those with competitive enrollment, have two application deadlines: one for early and one for regular admission. For most schools, the rate of admission is higher for early admission applications dates than for the regular admission deadline. Applying to your top choice schools during the early admission period can give you a better chance of gaining admission to that college if you prepare your application well. However, a well-prepared regular admission application will raise your chances far more than a poorly prepared, rushed, early admission application.

Most early decision applications are due at the end of October or November 1st. Students are allowed one "Early Decision" school, which you are obligated to attend if you are accepted. Your "early decision" school should be your top pick. (If you cannot obtain sufficient funding for that school, your obligation to attend is voided.) The CSS financial aid form is required for a few of the "early decision" schools in November. I recommend that students apply to their top choice school as their early decision school and a backup public school in their Haloween date appliction. It does not hurt to submit your applicaton to other schools early, since you will have completed the Common App and have gotten your letters of recommendations already completed.

Also in September, map out application deadlines for scholarships on your calendar. While most scholarship deadlines for high school seniors are in the spring, many are much earlier. The deadline for the Coca-Cola Scholarship ($10,000 to $20,000) is November 1.

The Federal Financial aid forms (the FAFSA) should be completed by mid February if applying financial aid for the fall of 2015 or 2016. If applying for financial aid for the fall of 2017 or after, the applications will be available and should be done in October of the preceding year. Any private colleges you have applied to will also want the CSS by February, although your early choice college usually will ask for it in November.

All that we are is the result of what we have thought. The mind is everything. What we think we become.

~Buddha

APPENDIX B: MATH TIPS AND TRAPS

Life is not about discovering our talents; it is about pushing our talents to the limit and discovering our genius.

~Robert Brault

For the SAT and ACT, you need to work quickly and accurately.

- Read the question carefully; answer what is asked, not what may look like the question at first glance.
- Know the math terms and vocabulary.
- Even though a mast test, avoid doing unneeded calculations.
- Avoid using a calculator.

Many questions depend on knowing math terms and number definitions. A *rational number* is the quotient (the result of division) of a fraction made up of two *integers* (whole numbers). Thus, 6/7 and 7/3 are rational numbers, but there cannot be a zero in the denominator. The square root of a prime number, *pi*, *e*, and most possible numbers are *irrational numbers*. Anything on a number line (negative, zero or positive number, rational or irrational is a *real number*.

To increase your speed, first learn how to solve the questions, then work on accuracy. Next, continue practice, which will build confidence, and then speed will come on its own. The ACT only allows one minute allotted per math question. After understand how to do the questions, practice with a clock.

Calculators are not needed for either the ACT or SAT, and for most questions, will slow you down. A calculator, such as the TI-84, may be programmed to solve certain problem quickly, but don't expect it to help if you have not practiced testing with it. Make sure your calculator is one permitted for use with the test. If you plan to use programmed formulas, make sure to use them during practice tests. Using them as a crutch at the last minute will likely trip you up. Sharing calculators is prohibited during tests. Ensure that the batteries are good before the test. Some helpful programs are given in the "Boost your ACT" program.

My mother had a degree in mathematics, and she taught me to love little numbers. In algebra, using 1's, 2's, 3's and 4's can simplify most problems to child's play, as they are easy to wrap your head around and understand. Additionally, using the number 1 for x in algebraic problems eliminates multiplication and possible multiplication errors. If you want to solve a problem or check an answer, use small numbers for algebraic questions for the unknowns. Turn your x's and y's into little numbers to see if it works. Even when you don't know how to solve a problem, you can often just plug in 1's and 2's for x and y, for example, and eliminate wrong answers.

If you give x the value of 1 in a problem it may be solved with fewer steps. For example, if 1 is used for x, $y=5x$ becomes $y=5$.

The number zero can also be used for x or another variable if the question does not call for a non-zero integer. For questions that ask for any number, do not forget negative numbers.

If x does not equal zero, then which of the following must be true?

1. $x^2 > x$	2. $2x > x$	3. $x+1 > x$

a)   1
b)   2
c)   3
d)   1 and 3 only
e)   1, 2, and 3

Here if you use $x=2$ as an example then answer e; *all three* appear true, looks correct. However, if you use x= -1, you find that only answer c is correct.

Many math problems on the college placement tests can be solved through brute force. Of five possible answers, four are wrong. Thus, if you have some time, but don't know how to approach a problem, plug in the numbers given in the answers. If the numbers are an array of values, pick the number in the middle of the range of answers. If it is wrong and is too high a number, for example, then one of the two lower numbers has to be correct. At this point, you can work the problem again if there is time and either get the right answer or hopefully, eliminate the wrong one. Even if you eliminate one wrong answer, you can raise your chances to getting points.

Math Traps

Most of the math on the SAT and ACT can be solved with simple algebra, or even middle school math. Nevertheless, be careful; there are many tricks to catch those who jump at the obvious answers. Don't fall for the following traps:

Rates: Don't average rates (speeds)
Averages: Don't average averages
Percentages: Don't add or subtract percentages

Martha drove west to her workplace from her home at 30 miles per hour and then returned home driving east at 60 miles per hour. What was her average speed?

Rates: It sure looks easy to take the average and get 45 mph, but that is wrong. If we assume she drove one unit (one hour) west she drove 30 miles at 30 mph, and then home 30 miles at 60 mph, which would take 30 minutes. She thus drove for a total of 60 miles in 90 minutes. Since 90 minutes is 1.5 hours, dividing the 60 miles by 1.5, results in an average rate of 40 mph.

Percentages and Averages: For algebraic problems with percentages, it is often helpful to use *x=100* if you are going to work the problem. One common trap is a problem that may appear to be easily solved by adding or subtracting two percentages. Don't add or subtract percentages. Similarly, don't average averages.

The 25 students in 2nd period had an average test score of 80 percent, while the 15 students in 3rd period averaged 90 percent on the same test. What was the overall average test score?

The bait in the trap is to guess 85% and move on. If you think about it, you can see that the larger class should be weighted more heavily, and thus the true average will be between 85% (the average if both classes had the same number of students) and 80%. Sometimes you will need no more information than this to answer the question.

To solve, multiply 0.8 x 25 =20, and .9 x 15 = 13.5. Add the products (20 + 13.5 = 35.5) and then divide this by the total number of students (40). Thus, 35.5/40 = 83.75%.

Integers between Points Trap

How many days are there <u>between</u> Monday and Friday? (3)
How many integers are <u>between</u> 5 and 50? (49-5=44)
How many days are there <u>from</u> June 5th until June 7th? (Two days, June 5th and 6th)

Pay attention to the words: <u>Between</u> is the number not including the variables, while <u>from</u> one point to another is the difference.

Ratio:ratio:ratio traps

Given ratios A:B and B:C, what is the ratio of A:C?

If the ratio of red to yellow is 5:2 and the ratio of yellow to blue is 3:4, what is the ratio of red to blue?

For this type of problem, "B" (yellow) needs to be converted to the same value for both ratios.

Red to yellow (A to B = 5:2) multiplied times 3 is 15:6
Yellow to blue (B to C = 3:4) multiplied times 2 is 6:8
Now that yellow (B) has the same value (6), it can be seen that the red:blue ratio is 15:8, which is equal to 1.875:1

Triangles to Know

The Pythagorean Theorem states that the square of the length of the hypotenuse (the side opposite the 90° angle) of a right triangle is equal to the sum of the squares of the other two sides. There are a few right triangles that have simple numeric relationships that make them easy to calculate, and thus they are often used in math tests, such as the ACT and SAT. If you recognize these triangles you can save time on the test and simplify your tasks of calculating answers.

Triangles give constant relationships. Thus, in the first triangle below, the 45°:45°:90° triangle, which is a square cut diagonally, the two adjacent sides are the same, and the hypotenuse is the length of a side times the square root of 2; about 1.414. Thus, for any 45°:45°:90° the hypotenuse can be calculated as (side * $\sqrt{2}$). If the side of a square is 21, then the diagonal will be 21 * $\sqrt{2}$).

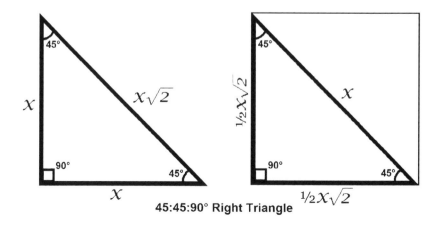

45:45:90° Right Triangle

Since the sides are equal in this special triangle, the formula $a^2 + b^2 = c^2$ can be written as $2a^2 = c^2$, and thus sides adjacent to the right angle can be calculated from the hypotenuse as $a^2 = \frac{1}{2}c^2$. It follows that if the hypotenuse, $c = 1$, then side, $a = \frac{1}{2}\sqrt{2}$. For any $45°:45°:90°$ triangle or square, the sides will equal the length of the hypotenuse $* \frac{1}{2}\sqrt{2}$; about $c * 0.707$. On a test, the answer is more likely to be expressed as $\frac{1}{2}x * \sqrt{2}$.

Examples:

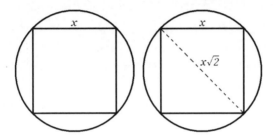

In the circle is a square, which has a side with a length of x. From the 45:45:90 triangle rule, we know that the diameter of the circle will be $x\sqrt{2}$. From this, we can find the radius, area, and circumference of the circle.

The next triangle to know is the $30°: 60°: 90°$ right triangle.

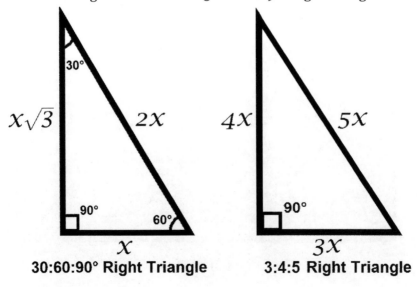

30:60:90° Right Triangle   3:4:5 Right Triangle

The sides opposite to the angles are as follows:

- The length of the side opposite to 30° = x
- The length of the side opposite to 60° = x√3
- The length of the side opposite to 90° = 2x

Any right triangle with a hypotenuse twice as long as one of the sides is a 30°: 60°: 90° triangle.

Another triangle of note is the 3:4:5 right triangle. It appears on tests as it provides nice, simple, round number answers. Since 3^2 + 4^2 = 5^2, it neatly demonstrates the Pythagorean theorem. But don't expect it to be this obvious. Since the relationship of side-lengths are constant, this triangle may also be a 6:8:10 or 9:12:15 or any $3x:4x:5x$ multiple triangle. It could also appear in fraction forms for example: $(3/3):(4/3):(5/3)$. Thus, in the proportions might be expressed as:

$$x : 4/x : 5/x \quad \text{or} \quad x/3 : x : x5 \quad \text{or} \quad x/5 : x/4 : x$$

Tip: A right triangle lives within any triangle, and equilateral triangles (60°: 60°: 60°) can be divided into two 30:60:90 right triangles, to calculate the height, and sides of the triangle.

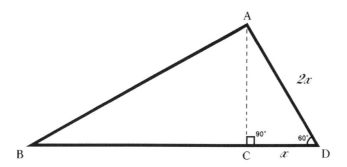

Example: What is the area of triangle ABD? In the triangle above, segment CD has a length of x, side AD of $2x$. Since this is a 30°: 60°: 90° triangle, we know that if the side AD has a length of $2x$, side BD, the hypotenuse of the triangle, must have a length of $4x$.

The area of a triangle is height times base, divided by two. We know from the 30°: 60°: 90° triangle rule, that the height of the triangle AC is x√3. The base is given as 4x.

Volume of triangle ABD = $x\sqrt{3} \cdot 4x \cdot \frac{1}{2} = 2x^2\sqrt{3}$

Formula for the sum of the interior angles of a polygon: (Number of sides of the polygon − 2) * 180

The square root of 2 ≈ 1.414...
The square root of 3 ≈ 1.732...
The square root of 5 ≈ 2.236...

Trig for Dummies

The ACT tests contain three simple one difficult trig question. The knowledge base required for the easy ones is provided here. If you don't know trig, this may seem very confusing until you use this information on a few practice tests and see how simple and useful it can be.

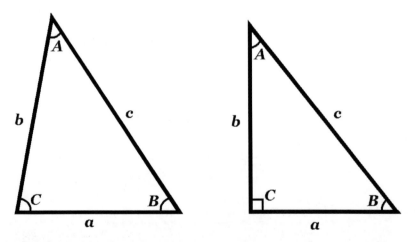

Cosine: The cosine law states: $c^2 = a^2 + b^2 − (2ab \cdot cosine\ of\ angle\ C)$. Don't worry about calculations; this is easy. You only need only to know what the formula looks like, as the test will not ask you to calculate the answer. Here is what you need to know: In a triangle, when two sides are known, the length of the unknown side of the triangle can be calculated from the two known sides (side a and side b) and the angle between a and b (angle C). Your job will be to find the value of angle C.

   Therefore, for the triangle a, b, c, with sides a and b, and angle C known, the formula for the length of c will look like this:

$$c = \sqrt{a2 + b2 - 2ab \cos C°}$$

Sine: The law of sines can be used to compute the third side length of a triangle when two angles and a side are known.

According to the law $\quad \dfrac{a}{\sin A} \quad = \quad \dfrac{b}{\sin B} \quad = \quad \dfrac{c}{\sin C}$

   In the special case of a right triangle, where C is a 90° angle, and c is the hypotenuse: sin A= a/c, and sin B = b/c. This can also be rearranged to solve a, b, or c:

$$a = \sin A \bullet c \quad \text{and} \quad C = a/\sin A.$$

Tangent: Tangents are used in trigonometry to find the remaining sides and angles when two sides and the enclosed angle are known. Knowing this alone is sometimes enough to answer the question.

Mnemonic for right triangles in trig: SOH CAH TOA
Sin=Opposite/ Hypotenuse: Sin A = a/c and Sin B = b/c
Cos=Adjacent/Hypotenuse: Cos A = b/c and Cos B = a/c
Tan=Opposite/Adjacent: TanA = a/b and Tan B = b/a

As an example, for a right triangle where C is the right angle: Tan A = a/b can be rearranged: (a = Tan A • b) to calculate the length of side a. Use the tangent of angle A multiplied times the length of side b. Additionally, Tan A = Sin A/Cos A.

You never lose by loving. You always lose by holding back.
~Barbara De Angelis

APPENDIX B: LANGUAGE SECTION

Know yourself and you will win all battles.

~Sun Tzu

English Section

The gold standard for language and writing on the college placement tests is simple, clear, concise communication. The test asks you to identify changes that improve a sentence or paragraph. Look for changes that make the language more consistent, clarify the idea, and remove redundancy.

Paragraphs should convey a single concept. The introductory and summary sentences of the paragraph should be consistent with the main idea of the paragraph. Every sentence in a paragraph should support the concept being conveyed.

TIP: Spot the error questions: *There is no error in about 15% of the "spot the error" questions*. Thus, on average, about one in seven questions will have "No Change" as the correct answer.

Punctuation and grammar

If you are not a grammar wizard, learning grammar and punctuation is the easiest place to pick up points on the placement tests. On the ACT test, there are ten punctuation questions and a dozen grammar questions. Questions on punctuation will include commas, apostrophes, and occasionally semicolons. It is worth your time to learn the rules of grammar and punctuation that appear on these tests. Knowing them not only helps on college prep tests, but also will help your writing and grades throughout high school, college, and beyond.

Following, some of the more common grammar and punctuation difficulties encountered in English are given; many of these are used on college prep tests. Not all of these occur on tests, especially when two different forms are considered correct. They are reviewed here as they are worth knowing and can help avoid confusion.

Confusing Apostrophes

Its and It's: Contractions rule in the world of apostrophes. Thus, "it is" becomes "*it's*" while "its" is the possessive of it. *He's* and *she's* are contractions of "he is" and "she is," while *his* and *her* are the possessive. "*You're*" is the contraction of "you are," while "*your*" is the possessive. "*Who's*" means who is, while "*whose*" is the possessive.

An apostrophe followed by an "*s*" also shows possession: *The collision damaged Tom's car.*

If the word is a plural ending in "*s*", the apostrophe comes after:

The workers' office was damaged in a storm.

Be careful of words that are already plurals (such as men, women and children) without the "s" to denote a plural. For these, use an apostrophe followed by "s" for possessive:

The children's school was also damaged.

If a person's name or a noun ends in the letter "s," then the apostrophe can go after the "s" or an extra apostrophe "s" can be added. Either way is correct. If the name or noun ending in "s" has two or more syllables, it is more common to just add an apostrophe as it sounds better: Mr. Rodgers's sounds wrong.

- *Miss Jones' recital went well.*
- *Mr. Jones's car crashed into a tree.*
- *The glass's color changed.*

- *Chris's brother likes popcorn.*
- *Doris's cat chases cars.*
- *Dr. Lewis's book is brilliantly written.*
- *Mr. Rodgers' cat ran away.*

Apostrophes are also used to make letters or single numbers plural: *I earned four A's and two B's this semester.*

Commas and Coordinating Conjunctions

Coordinating conjunctions, also called coordinators, are conjunctions that join two or more items of *equal syntactic importance*, such as words, main clauses, or sentences. Coordinating conjunctions are used, for example, to join two sentences into a single sentence.

Commas precede coordinating conjunctions: for, and, nor, but, or, yet, so. The mnemonic acronym *FANBOYS* is often taught to help remember the more common coordinating conjunctions:

For presents a reason: *"She is dieting to lose weight, for her doctor has diagnosed her as having diabetes."*
And presents non-contrasting item(s) or idea(s): *"They overeat, and they gain weight."*
Nor presents a non-contrasting negative idea: *"She does not smoke, nor does she drink."*
But presents a contrast or exception: *" She worked out three times a week, but was unable to lose any weight. "*
Or presents an alternative item or idea: *"She walks to work, or she rides her bike."*
Yet presents a contrast or exception: *"They diet, yet they don't exercise."*
So presents a consequence: *"He pulled a double shift yesterday, so he slept in this morning."*

The Serial Comma

Commas are also used to separate units in a list. Each unit gets a comma. In journalism, such as newspapers using small columns, the comma before *"or"* & *"and"* are generally omitted to save space. Writing is usually clearer with the comma, so it should be used.

The lawyer, a thief and a conman, walked into the courtroom.
The lawyer, a thief, and a conman walked into the courtroom.
The lawyer, a thief and a conman walked into the courtroom.

In the first example, the lawyer is a thief and a conman. This sentence has an independent clause describing the lawyer. In the 2nd and 3rd examples example is one or more serial commas are correctly used, but the 3rd sentence is unclear as to what is happening. Since either the second or third form may be used, the college placement tests do not test on this.

The music store carried guitars, trumpets, drums, and banjos.

People often become confused when the units are bigger, but the rule still applies:

The party was attended by a knight in armor, cooks, scullery maids, the crown prince's entourage of hooligans, and fifteen ladies-in-waiting.

The Semicolon

One of the most feared punctuation marks is the semicolon; it connects ideas that are related, although different. Usually, a FANBOYS is used to connect two sentences into one, but if you don't want to use a coordinating conjunction, a semicolon can be used instead. Semicolons are also used just before conjunctive adverbs to tie pairs of phases together. Some examples of conjunctive adverbs include, therefore, thus, nevertheless, likewise, still, additionally, and consequently.

Remember that a full sentence lives on either side of a semicolon, and a pronoun in the second sentence phrase usually replaces the noun from the first sentence phrase. The writer could have used two sentences; however, the semicolon ties the two ideas together more closely.

Alex hated his job; he spent his workdays doing boring, repetitive tasks.
She said that Jack was like perfect chocolate; he was dark, sweet, and rich.
Lasagna is one of my favorite dishes; nevertheless, I ordered the seafood casserole when we ate a Mario's restaurant.

Semicolons are also used between items in a series when one or more of these items includes commas. Thus, they function as "super commas" for lists of lists.

I lived on a farm with goats, pigs, and ducks; broken-down tractors; miles of fences in need of repair; and dogs named Zeus and Athena.

Colons

The most common use of the colon is to inform the reader that the information following the colon proves, explains, or lists elements of what preceded it. Colons can be used between independent clauses if the second clause summarizes or explains the first one. Colons can be thought of as an equal sign where the part after the comma explains the first part.

There were only four items available on the menu: tripe, fried kidney, grilled liver, and Rocky Mountain oysters.

The colon can be used to introduce the logical consequence or effect, of the fact that is stated.

There was only one choice left: run away or stay and live in shame.
Sam was exhausted: he could walk no farther.
Sally spent her workdays doing boring, repetitive tasks: she hated her job.

For the last two sentences, it would not have been incorrect to use semicolons, however the colon indicates that second phrase is a logical outcome of the first sentence phrase, rather than that they are only related. In the sentence below, there is no causation or equality of the phrases.

He was exhausted; home was still miles away.

Correlative Conjunctive Pairs

There are six pairs to know. Avoid mixing and match.
1. Whether...or
2. Either...or
3. Neither ... nor
4. Not only...but...also
5. Both...and
6. Just as...so

<u>Not only</u> am I handsome, <u>but</u> I am <u>also</u> brilliant.

Verb Tense

The word *tense* refers to the timing of the action of the verb. While simple past, present, and future tense are straight forward, students often make errors with other forms.

Habitual Actions: Present Tense

Use the simple present for any habitual action. These are things done on a regular basis.
I go to work every Monday morning.
We attend church on Fridays.
Sam enjoys milk with his cookies.

Progressive Tense

The progressive tense is used for anything that is happening. Progressive tenses are easy to spot because their verbs always end with "-ing" and are used with a helping verb. A helping verb is used just so that we know who and when we are describing. In the present progressive, the helping verbs are the present tense conjugations of "to be."

I am sitting and typing at my computer.
I was sleeping soundly when lightening struck.
I will be earning a higher salary in my new job.

Perfect Tense

The perfect tense is used to describe things that have already occurred, but the time in which they occurred is considered unfinished. The perfect uses a past form of a verb with the verb "to have."

Aaron had drunk the bitter cup of hatred for many years.
He had endured enslavement for far too long.
"I have been hungry for days," he moaned.
He will have wasted all of his inheritance gambling before the night is through.

Perfect Progressive Tense

When both the action and the time are considered unfinished, the verb combines a helping verb ("to be" and "to have") with the progressive form.

They had been drinking all night.
"I will be watching you," warned the detective.
She is wearing the same skirt as Mary is.

Singular and Plural Confusion

On the test, look for subject–verb number agreement
1. Prepositional phrases
2. Group nouns
3. Tricky singulars

1. The prepositional phrase may trick you. These are phrases stuck in the middle of sentences, which may cause confusion.

This box, one out of thousands, contain a prize.
The children, including my child, likes ice cream.

Only one out of thousands of boxes contain a prize, but here the sentence is about "This box." "*This box <u>contains</u> a prize*" would be correct. Be careful not to confuse the number in the independent clause inserted into the middle of a sentence with a number in the subject and verb. These are simple examples and easy to see, but this can be trickier in long, complex sentences.

Lady Marion, accompanied by Robin and Will Scarlet, quietly walks through the forest, evading the sheriff.

2. Group nouns that are singular can also be tricky.

The group of friends go to the theater on Saturday evening every weekend.

While *friends* are plural, group is singular. The subject is group. Thus, *"The group (of friends) goes to the theater"* is correct. Other examples of singular group nouns include flock, school of fish, pride of lions, data, class of new students.

3. Tricky singulars: Anyone, anything, someone, everyone, everything. These are singular. Make sure the verb is in singular form. Additionally *all of, most of, some of, any of, and none of* are singular when understood as a single group. *Everyone, anyone, each,* and *everybody* are singular when they describe a single group.

> *Everyone needs to take a vacation.* (Singular)
> *All workers need to take vacations.* (Plural)
> *Everyone wants to be loved.* (Singular)
> *Each of the children needs sandals for the beach.* (Singular)
> *Most of the class is learning the material, but some of the students are failing.* (Singular followed by plural)

Dropped Verbs

> *She is smarter than me.*
>   a.   than me
>   b.   than I.

Here the correct answer is "than I." The reason is that the unabbreviated, complete sentence is: "She is smarter than I am."

The Faulty Adverb or Adjective

Make sure that an adverb is used to describe a verb and that an adjective is used to describe a noun.

Matt tried real hard to get the ball through the hoop.

Here the word real is modifying the verb *tried* and thus should be an adverb, but real is an adjective. Adverbs commonly end in *"ly"*. Changing to "tried really hard" corrects this sentence.

After dating two sisters, I decided I liked the blond one best.
The word *"best"* here acts as an adverb modifying the verb "liked." *"Best"* is a multiple superlative, and thus, should be used to limit one of at least three choices. In this sentence, *"I liked the blond one better"* would be correct; however, changing "two" to "three" sisters would correct the sentence.

Not all adverbs end in "ly." Now, soon, and yesterday can be adverbs when they describe when the verb's action occurs. Superlatives also act as adverbs: *much, more, most; a little, less, least; soon, sooner, soonest; well, better, best; badly, worse, worst; far, further (farther), furthest (farthest); fast, faster, fastest.*

I hope that you are feeling better.

Better modifies or refines the verb, feeling.

Subjective and Objective Pronouns

The subjective pronoun is used for the subject of action. The objective pronoun is used for a person or object affected by or receiving the action.

Subject Pronoun	Verb	Object Pronoun
I	hit	him.
She	kissed	me.
They	robbed	us.
We	defeated	them.
I	helped	her.
(The person) who	helped	us, ...
It	offended	whom?

Who and *whoever* are subject pronouns while *whom* and *whomever* are object pronouns. In the sentence: "*The man, whom I hit, fell to the ground,*" whom I hit could be rearranged to "I hit him." If it is difficult to decide whether to use who or whom, look to see who is acting. The actor is the subject.

My cousin and me went to the store.
      a.   cousin and me
      b.   cousin and I

Since the pronoun is being used as a subject, the correct choice is "My cousin and I."

TRICK: Try dropping the extra person from the sentence. You would never say "Me went to the store."

Parallelism

In improving sentence problems, look for sentences which do not use parallel forms. When a sentence contains two or more items linked by "and" or "or," those items are parallel; therefore, should be expressed in the same grammatical form.

John likes camping, fishing, and to hunt.

Here there is a mix of verb tense. Use just one form.
  John likes camping, fishing, and hunting.
  John likes to camp, fish, and hunt.
  "*The old man drove slowly and with caution,*" would be improved if written as "*The old man drove slowly and cautiously.*"

She passed the day swimming, lying on the beach and read a book. Changing the sentence to "*reading a book*" would be better.

Correlative conjunction pairs (not only/but also, either/or, neither/nor, both/and,) should also have parallel comparisons

The protestors not only <u>want freedom</u>, but also <u>to be equal</u>.

This sentence would be improved if written as: *The protestors not only <u>want freedom</u>, but also <u>want equality</u>.*
You are either <u>with us</u> or <u>you are with those</u> who would destroy America! would be better written as: *You are either <u>with us</u> or <u>with those</u> who would destroy America!*

"I am neither <u>a nihilist</u> nor <u>am I a Pollyannaish optimist</u>." This would be better revised as "I am neither <u>a nihilist</u> nor <u>a Pollyannaish optimist</u>."

John awoke to see <u>IVs in his arms, a cast on his leg</u>, and <u>a headache</u> like never before. This is an illogical comparison. It would be better as two sentences. *John awoke to see <u>IVs in his arms</u> and <u>a cast on his leg</u>. He had a headache like never before.*

To be nobody but yourself, in a world which is doing its best night and day, to make you everybody else, means to fight the hardest battle which any human being can fight; and never stop fighting.

~e.e. cummings

Inspiration exists, but it has to find you working.

~Pablo Picasso

APPENDIX C: READING SECTION

You gain strength, courage and confidence by every experience in which you really stop to look fear in the face.

~Eleanor Roosevelt

For many people, the reading section is the most onerous part of the placement tests. However, steps can be taken to tame it.

The ACT reading section allows only 35 minutes for 40 questions. There are four reading passage of about 750 words, accompanied by ten questions relating to each passage. Thus, the test allows less than nine minutes per section. This tight time constraint makes this test difficult. It's a race. To do well on reading the sections, the time allotted must be used effectively.

The trick is to read the passage at a comfortable pace, neither too intensely nor trying to skim through, to skimp on time. Haste makes waste. If you read too quickly, you will waste time as you will end up rereading and searching for answers. If you read too slowly, you will run out of time and may be distracted by detail, rather than the larger concepts, which are the subject of most questions. You want to see the forest, not the mites living in the moss growing on the bark of the trees. The secret, and goal of practice, is to learn to read at a level of intensity and speed that allows you to acquire the information required to answer the questions correctly and finish on time.

As you practice these tests, try to pace your reading so that it takes under four minutes to read the passage. A reading speed of about 200 to 230 words a minute allows the 750-word passage to be read in 3¼ to 3¾ minutes. This is the most effective reading rate to provide a level of understanding needed for most literature and journalism, and to answer the questions on the ACT and SAT reading tests.

When training for this section, avoid rereading, or doubling back, to reread lines. Sentences are made up of concept phrases. Many people reread phrases, when sections of a sentence are not clear. Often, concepts are spread over more than one line. Rereading the first section of an incomplete concept will not help, but rather, breaks up concentration and slows reading. When you practice, do not allow yourself to reread; trust that you will achieve understanding by reading through the next set of words.

Avoid reading word by word, as this greatly slows reading and diminishes comprehension and memory of the passage. Read by saccade, where the eyes hop across the line. This book's layout was designed for easy reading, using three to four hops per line, each saccade taking in clusters of 15 to 20 letters at a time. The ACT has about 53 letters per line. An average line should be read using about three saccades, although word length, sentence structure, and punctuation affect saccade size.

Good drivers slow down for curves, potholes, and other hazards. Do the same in reading. Slow down for unfamiliar words and concepts, and speed up for easy sections. Memory and comprehension are better when reading at a quick pace than at a slow one. When reading more slowly, the mind begins to multitask and wander off into the vapor. This is not an effective strategy for a placement test where your future rides on answering each question in less than 30 seconds.

If, after practice, you still have difficulty reading the passages with sufficient comprehension within 4 minutes, you may benefit from training with a speed-reading software program. These programs help train the eyes to move effectively for reading and improve comprehension. Some recommended speed reading programs are listed in Chapter 6. They work most effectively when used in practice for at least 15 minutes each day. Most of these programs allow entry of sample passages into the program for training. For the ACT or SAT, train to read at high comprehension, at a rate of 220 to 230 words per minute.

Practicing the reading section, by paying attention to the appropriate level of focus required to answer the questions, will help you tune your reading speed to do well on this section. Technical writing, such as found in the ACT science section, may warrant slightly slower reading, around 200 words per minute.

In the reading sections, you will likely run into sentences with difficult wording that escapes comprehension. Don't allow this to become a distraction. Keep reading, as these sentences likely will not cripple the overall understanding required to answer the questions.

The Four Passages

Section 3 of the ACT is a reading test with four passages and four corresponding sets of questions. They appear in the following order:
1. Prose – Fiction
2. Social Science
3. Humanities
4. Natural Science

Each section type requires a slightly different tact.

Prose: The prose section is the only fiction section on the test. It is important to get a sense of mood and tone. Who is narrating the story? Are they objective or biased? Who are main characters? Who does what, and in what sequence? Is there a conflict? Is the conflict internal or external? What change takes place in the characters?

The prose sections often use metaphors, understatement or hyperbole, and poetic language. Thus, the section requires interpretation. It is not a simple find-a-word-in-a-passage puzzle. These passages require interpretation of the prose. For this section, I do not find pre-reading of the questions helpful.

Nonfiction Sections: For the non-fiction passages, reading the questions (but not the answers) before you read the passage may help you focus on the elements that will be asked. Many people find that underlining key elements in the section as they read helps them focus on main points.

Social Science: Pay attention to organization, cause and effect relationships, comparisons, and chronological order. Look for the main idea.

Humanities: These are expository or descriptive, usually non-fiction, prose. They often focus on the arts. Look for the main idea. Note supporting details. Look for cause/effect relationships. Pay attention to why something is happening and who or what is responsible. What core idea is the author promoting?

Natural Science: This passage focuses on concepts, details, generalizations, and theories. How do the concepts relate to larger ideas? Look for organizational patterns. Note the main idea and supporting details. Look at how things are compared with each other.

Answering Questions

Cause and Effect: Questions may ask about causation, effect, and organizational patterns. Pay attention while reading for clues that indicate transitions:

- Causation: therefore, because, consequently, resulting from,
- Comparison: Similarly, likewise, more, less
- Sequence or order: first, second, next, finally, time or date
- Enumeration: firstly, secondly, finally.

Inference: If the tests ask what is *stated* in the passage, they are asking what is literally written in the passage. The answer will usually not be a word-for-word statement, but rather will paraphrase what has been presented. If the question asks what the writer *implies,* it is asking what is hinted, but *not explicitly stated* in the passage. Imply means to hint, insinuate, or suggest.

When a question asks what the author *implies or suggests*, or asks which statement is *best supported*, you are being asked to draw conclusions about what the author hints is true, but does not come out and say directly. You need to make an inference, use reason to make a conclusion, or otherwise deduce *from the information in the passage* that something is true, even though not explicitly stated by the writer.

In addition to *imply,* and *suggest,* other phrases may also tell you that the test is asking for an inference. If the question asks you to determine what was in the mind of the author, it is asking you to make an inference. Look for questions with phrases similar to:

The author would likely agree
The author would most likely add

For inference questions, you want to be one step from the stated information, using only information from the passage without using any outside knowledge you may have on the topic.

Main Idea: The main idea is the overall purpose of the passage. It is the big picture. Look for the overall theme that is included throughout the passage, especially in the first and last paragraphs. Think how you would answer the question before you read the answer choices. Wrong answers will include:

• Too Narrow: An answer that accurately describes one paragraph, viewpoint, or feature or the passage, but not the big picture. Avoid answers that are too narrow and that describe just one aspect of the passage.
• Too Broad: Another typical wrong answer will assert something related, however not actually included in the passage. It may suggest an aspect of the topic that was not in the passage.

- Opposite: Watch out for an answer that asserts the reverse of the author's thesis. This one may be the most straightforward summation, and can sound right, but be the opposite. It may thus act as a clue to the real answer.

Author's Purpose: The author's purpose is different from the main idea. It is not what was said, but rather the author's motivation for writing. The answer will not be because his editor paid him to write it, or to get an A in her history class. The reason may be that the author wants to share their perspective, describe how they were changed, change the reader's point of view, or educate the reader on the topic. Sometimes the author wants to contrast or compare, to show the difference in ideas or things. Sometimes they want to criticize, or to suggest a new idea. They may want to illustrate or paint a picture that shows a deeper meaning. They may want to explain and simplify a complex idea.

Similar to the main idea, this will be an overall purpose, neither an item from a single paragraph nor something outside of the passage. Look for an answer that describes a global purpose.

Strategies

Final Paragraph: Pay particular attention to the concluding paragraph, as it usually contains a summary of the main thesis of the author.

Vocabulary and Word Meaning: If you don't know a vocabulary word, you can often figure out the right answer by reading the sentence and substituting each of the answer choices into the sentence to see which best correlates to the rest of the intent of the sentence and paragraph.

TIPS:
- Read every answer before making your decision, line through answers you know cannot be correct. Don't obliterate the

answers, however, because you still want to be able to read the answer in case you read wrong.

- Look for the best answer, as more than one may be correct.
- Watch out for exception questions (EXCEPT and NOT) where three of the answers are true, and only one is false. It is easy to overlook that the question is asking for the untrue statement and go with the first true statement you see.
- When you read the questions, don't look at the answers until you first think of what it should be. Then look for that answer. You are less likely to be tricked into a wrong answer.
- Answer the general questions first, followed by those referring to line numbers.
- So long as you are not running out of time, mark the answers for each passage in the booklet as you work, then copy the group of 10 answers for the passage onto the answer sheet before moving on. Don't leave any blank circles on the answer sheet when moving to the next reading passage.

TRAPS:
- Beware of answers that use extreme language. "Most," "best," and "only" are example of exclusionary terms. Watch out for exclusionary terms in questions. Life is not black or white, and accurate descriptions are rarely extremely narrow except in math.
- Beware of answers that depend on information included in the answer but which did not appear in the passage.
- Beware of answers that are outside of the scope of the passage.
- Beware of answers that repeat the exact language from the passage; they are usually part of a trick answer.

Often, the most obvious answer to the question will be attached to the wrong individual in the story, or be worded opposite to what is included in the passage. The test writers make the answer close to word-for-word of what is stated in the passage, but reverse the effect or change the character. Don't fall for it.

After you practice and score a few placement tests, you should have a good idea of which reading section types are easiest or most difficult for you. A couple of weeks before the exam, decide which type of reading section takes you the most time and which you score lowest on, especially if you tend to run out of time during this section. *When you take the real test, do the reading sections easiest for you first, and the save the most difficult for last*. This may give you extra time on the hardest parts without sacrificing the easy parts, or if you are running out of time, guess at the harder questions or one you have not had time to complete. Bring a watch to the test so you can keep track of how much time you have. The SAT test allows enough time for most people to complete the test, however, it asks more complex questions.

Review the directions from the actual practice test a few days before the test. This way, you will not need to spend time reading the directions on the day of the test.

TIP: The author/title/source sentences at the beginning of the passage do not contain any information needed in answers. You can ignore them to save time.

While this book provides some strategies for preparing for placement tests, it not meant as a complete guide or as your only source of guidance. The author's main purpose for this section is to convince the reader that preparation can greatly improve test scores. Practicing sample and retired tests is an important part of preparation.

Our greatest glory is not in never falling but in rising every time we fall.

~Confucius

SUPPLEMENT: ONE LAST THING

Success isn't a result of spontaneous combustion. You must set yourself on fire.

~Arnold H. Glasow

Set up and contribute to a Roth IRA retirement account when you get your first paycheck. Huh? What! Am I nuts???

If a young person invests a few thousand dollars a year into a retirement account for 6 years before the age of 25 and then never adds another dime to their retirement account, they should expect retire with more financial wealth than if they wait to begin saving at age 26, and put the same amount in every year for the next 40 years. The compounded growth in value, which accrues after six years, is greater than the annual contribution for an IRA. Even better is to double the retirement fund by adding to it every year until you retire.

In 2015, the maximum IRA contribution is $5500 a year. If you invest $5000 a year in a Roth IRA from ages 18 to 23 (a total of $30,000), invest it in a broad stock index fund, and don't touch it again, if the stock market behaves as it has in the past, your account should be worth about $2.8 million by retirement age. You'd be able to draw out (tax-free) $23,000 a month to supplement social security without touching the principal. Currently, $635 is given to most retirees. Sadly, no one bothered to tell me this when I was young.

A simple, reasonable, long-term investment for someone who is not an investment junkie, is to ETF (exchange-traded funds) index funds that represent either small-cap or midcap value stocks or smaller technology index funds each year, reinvesting all dividends. This long-term strategy depends on leaving the investment alone and not meddling with it. Don't sell until the money is used for retirement. Many people do poorly in the stock market because they worry about their investments and sell at the worst possible moment. It is far better to buy and forget.

Some reasonable ETFs types are:

A. S&P MidCap 400 Value ETF, such as VOE, IVOV or IJJ
B. Small Cap Value ETF, such as VBR, RZV, IJS, or VIOV
C. Technology ETFs, such as QTEC, QQQ, or XLK
D. Biotech ETFs, such as XBI, BBH, IBB, or BIB

If you want simple, chose a value ETF and buy it every year. Small cap and value index funds give above average long-term returns. Tech and biotech can give great returns, but can also fall. If you would like to be clever and increase returns over the long run, split each year's contribution and buy one of either A or B and one of either C or D ETFs. Choose the one from each pair that has had poorer performance during the previous year, contributing in January of the year you will be earning money. This method helps you buy the index when it is relatively cheap, and thus increases long-term return. This method is for long-term growth and is intended as advice for a young person. It may not be the best strategy for someone nearing retirement age.

It's tough to make predictions, especially about the future.
~Yogi Berra

No one goes to heaven by being afraid of hell. One moves closer to God through mature love and kindness. No one achieves great things by avoiding risk or from fear of failure. It is through passion and action that we move forward.
~Charly Lewis

~ The End ~

You don't get to choose how you're going to die, or when. But, you can decide how you're going to live now.
~Joan Baez

254

About the Author: Dr. Lewis is a physician, researcher, author, and inventor of several patented medical devices. He is board certified in Preventive Medicine and Public Health. His research focuses on tertiary prevention of chronic disease. He has been a life-long educational activist and has served on several educational boards. His professional interests include neuroinflammatory disease and cognitive function.

---

[1] Axelsson J, Sundelin T, Ingre M, Van Someren EJ, Olsson A, Lekander M. Beauty sleep: experimental study on the perceived health and attractiveness of sleep deprived people. BMJ. 2010 Dec 14;341:c6614.

[2] Persistent cannabis users show neuropsychological decline from childhood to midlife. Meier MH, Caspi A, Ambler A, Harrington H, Houts R, Keefe RS, McDonald K, Ward A, Poulton R, Moffitt TE. Proc Natl Acad Sci U S A. 2012 Oct 2;109(40):E2657-64.

[3] http://www.higheredinfo.org/dbrowser/index.php?submeasure=25&year=2007&level=nation&mode=graph&state=0

[4] Assessing the effects of caffeine and theanine on the maintenance of vigilance during a sustained attention task. Foxe JJ, Morie KP, Laud PJ, Rowson MJ, de Bruin EA, Kelly SP. Neuropharmacology. 2012 Jun;62(7):2320-7.

[5] http://news.harvard.edu/gazette/story/2012/12/895-admitted-through-early-action/

[6] http://collegeapps.about.com/b/2012/10/20/early-admit-rates-for-the-ivy-league-class-of-2016.htm

[7] Attention-deficit hyperactivity disorder (ADHD) stimulant medications as cognitive enhancers. Advokat C, Scheithauer M. Front Neurosci. 2013 May 29;7:82.

[8] Hoyt, D. P. *Relationship between college grades and adult achievement: A review of the literature.* Iowa City: American College Testing Program Research Report No. 7, 1965.

[9] Harmon, L. R. The development of a criterion of scientific competence. In C. W. Taylor and F. Barron (Eds.), *Scientific creativity; Its recognition and development.* NYC: John Wiley & Sons, 1963, 44-52.

[10] Duckworth, A.L. & Quinn, P.D. (2009). Development and validation of the Short Grit Scale (GRIT–S). Journal of Personality Assessment, Vol 91(2), pp. 166-174.

[11] James M. Richards, Jr. and Sandra W. Lutz. Predicting Student Accomplishment in College from the Act Assessment Journal of Educational Measurement. Vol. 5, No. 1 (Spring, 1968), pp. 17-29

[12] N Mesko, T Bereczkei. Hairstyle as an adaptive means of displaying phenotypic quality. Human Nature, 2004

Front cover photo by Andres Rodriguez
Back cover: Florida State University. Photo by Charles Lewis

Made in the USA
Lexington, KY
21 May 2017